ISBN 978-1-331-15536-2
PIBN 10151591

1 MONTH OF
FREE
READING

at
www.ForgottenBooks.com

By purchasing this book you are eligible for one month membership to ForgottenBooks.com, giving you unlimited access to our entire collection of over 700,000 titles via our web site and mobile apps.

To claim your free month visit:
www.forgottenbooks.com/free151591

Similar Books Are Available from
www.forgottenbooks.com

CHRISTIAN RADICALISM,

BY

WILLIAM WITHINGTON.

'Ὁ ἁμαρτάνων ἔναντι τοῦ ποιήσαντος αὐτόν, ἐμπέσοι εἰς χεῖρας ἰατροῦ.

ECCLESIASTICUS.

'Ἡμεῖς αὐτοὶ ἐν ἑαυτοῖς στενάζομεν, εκδε-χόμενοι τὴν ἀπολύτρωσιν τοῦ σώματος ἡμῶν.

PAULUS.

BOSTON:

PRINTED BY PERKINS & MARVIN.

1836.

Entered according to Act of Congress in the year 1836,
By WILLIAM WITHINGTON,
in the Clerk's Office of the District Court of Massachusetts.

PREFACE.

The following work is partly original, and partly consisting of articles before published. It seemed necessary to republish these, in order to present fully the author's views; or else, to write anew the substance in another form; in which no important advantages were seen.

Some may think, I have discordantly mingled theological doctrines with other things. I can only say in self-defence, that I have endeavored to state what seemed to me truth, according to its connections in my own mind—to present my conclusions according to the trains of thought, by which I had arrived at them. The truth revealed by God in his word, and the truth disclosed by man's conduct as created for this life, seem to me to reflect the clearest light on each other: and I am conscious, that I should have apprehended neither with my present satisfaction, but for the help derived from a comparison of the two. I have endeavored to read the word of God, and to mark human conduct, for myself, unhampered by systems of divinity, or systems of philosophy. I have expressed my own sentiments fearlessly; without expecting to find any party ready to respond to them fully. Unless therefore the work should fall into the hands of an isolated reader, here and there, prepared for this; in consideration of what the reader may find to approve, I must crave his indulgence for the rest. I claim no peculiar credit for venturing upon such a work. If anywise fitted for it, it is because few, who have devoted much attention to passing objects of interest, have been kept less connected with, or less pledged to, any sect, party, or denomination; and this by that overruling

Divinity, which so often thwarts our wills, to shape our rough-hewn ends.

After all, my views of human conduct coincide with those, which the shrewdest observers have adopted independently of revelation. He who can talk with Brown of human virtue, must be acute only for the speculations of the closet. I know not, whether governor McDuffie be a very devout student of the Scriptures: for the following sentiment in his inaugural speech, might either have been learned from them, or from general history and observation.

"However melancholy the fact may be, all history is but a bloody testimony to establish it, that no community of men on the face of the earth, in any age, or under any dispensation, political or religious, ever has been governed by justice in its negotiations or conflicts with other states. No, gentlemen, it is not justice and magnanimity, but interest and ambition—dignified and disguised under the name of State Policy—that ever has governed, and ever will govern masses of men, acting as political communities."

His excellency's design did not lead him to speak of "masses of men," otherwise than as "political communities." But neither reason nor observation demands the restriction of the sentiment to masses acting in that capacity. His anticipation that it "ever will" be so, seems to justify the surmise, that he came to his conclusion more from the study of secular history, than of that volume, which declares, that "a king shall reign in righteousness, and princes shall rule in judgment."

The fact of this supreme preponderance of the selfish principle is quite consistent with another, that men generally are not conscious of designedly sacrificing all the best interests of others to their own selfish ends. The consciousness of so doing is too painful: they therefore generally contrive, but too successfully, to hide the plain truth from themselves. But though selfishness may generally operate first to pervert the judgment, it is not the less a reality. Did men love their neighbor as themselves, it would not be so. For the want of such love, and the consequences, they are fully responsible. Only in this negative or constructive sense, I suppose, did the apostle 'mean to characterize men, till born again, as "hateful and hating one another."

But here, men who agree upon the fact, differ as to the moral construction. They who will not admit the perfect reasonableness of God's demand to be loved with all the heart, and strength, and mind, and that man love his neighbor as himself, plead the incompetence of human infirmity to exercise fully such love, in mitigation of the sentence of condèmnation. In accordance with this, there is a vast deal of loose popular reasohing, as if, so far as the conduct of men may be certainly calculated on, so far as it may be resolved into laws invariably acting— they are not perfect moral agents—they cannot rightly be held strictly accountable for every deviation from the perfect law of God. But this resolving of transgression into the excusable necessity imposed by our constitution and circumstances, is really to throw the guilt upon God ; unless I have exerted my closest powers of analysis in vain.

May the time soon come, when it shall be generally and fully admitted, that the word of God contains the soundest and most practical philosophy of the human mind ; how miserably short-sighted selfishness overlooks the truest interest and the truest honor,* in its groveling search and eager grasp ; and how miserably we consult for the dignity of human nature, when we strive to exalt it, by evading the charges, which our Sovereign brings against us. This strife has ever resulted in our worse degradation. We accordingly see, that the men most actively and ardently engaged in vindicating man's true dignity, have been the men, who most scorned to glory in aught, save in the cross of our Lord Jesus Christ—who most fully admitted the conclusion, that if one died for all, then were all dead. Such have been the principles of the leading spirits in the capital revolutions for rescuing

---

* " He said to me after his return from abroad, that he *had* at some periods indulged hopes of such honors as our profession could afford, but that he had totally renounced all such hopes and wishes for that, which he deemed of much more importance, the being truly useful to his fellow men."—*Memoir of James Jackson, Jr., M. D.*

Alas ! that in any profession the highest honors should be considered as so distinct from the being truly useful to one's fellow men.

mankind from superstition and bondage. And however one may speculate, he hardly doubts, that such are the principles of him, who, to vindicate man's true dignity, forsakes kindred and home, and braves a polar winter, or a tropical sun, to raise intellects debased almost below the brutes to the dignity of reasonable, thinking, and adoring beings.

I must now request the reader to adopt practically the following sentiment from the Quarterly Christian Spectator, Vol. VI. p. 546. "He who loves truth will not be fastidious of the quarter whence it comes: and though it may seem contrary to his prejudices, though it may infringe on some venerable form of belief, or be opposed to much that passes for knowledge in the world; yet it will be welcomed, and its influence felt and allowed on the judgment and the life."

The remarks which follow in the Spectator, on the connection between holiness and independence of thought and advancement in truth, are well worthy of every reader's consideration.

I have discussed topics calculated to be exciting. Had it been my object to rouse popular indignation against men interested in the perpetuation of old abuses, and to puff myself into notoriety as a popular leader, I see abundant evidence, how easy would have been the undertaking: and this is only saying, that whoever undertakes to raise the bad passions of men, has a very easy task before him. If I have not *less*, I have not *such* ambition. I have been ambitious, (if such be the term,) to arouse public sentiment to demand some radical reforms, without cherishing viler passions than a sincere desire to see those by education the adherents of conservative principles brought into circumstances safer to their moral principles, and better for their ultimate welfare, even for this life. Whether I have made the attempt too early, remains to be seen. For the credit of the age, I hope not. As to my own credit in the attempt, I can cheerfully appeal to the ultimate decision of an intelligent people; and still more cheerfully to that tribunal, whither we are all hastening.

CHRISTIAN RADICALISM.

BODY AND SOUL.

No. I.

ONE principle pervading the institutions of
Moses is, that there is an intimate connection
between body and soul—that a foundation for
moral and religious improvement should be laid
in a careful attention to the constitution of the
human body, and the external agents affecting
it. I believe, that a vast number of his regula-
tions, which generally have been treated as ca-
pricious and frivolous, or more piously resolved
into the good pleasure and inexplicable will of
the Deity, or with more show of reason, referred
simply to the necessity of establishing some
arbitrary distinctions between the people of God
and the surrounding idolatrous nations, have
their foundation in the soundest philosophy of

human nature. I propose to show in a few instances, how institutions, generally considered as of temporary or inexplicable expediency, rest upon reasons as lasting as the constitution of nature.

Moses forbade to eat blood or fat. Nothing need be said of the former. As to the latter, it is found that disease in an animal affects the fat before the lean. The former may be diseased, while the latter may be eaten with comparative impunity. The regulation, too, was calculated to discourage the artificial and vicious manner of fattening animals now almost universally' practised. Where such a regulation was in force, people would be little likely to stall-fatten their cattle on a fermented mixture of chopped vegetables and meal, or have recourse to the various expedients for creating an artificial appetite, in order to load the animal speedily with artificial fat. Animals thus fattened are in fact diseased: and the owner calculates his *immediate* interest closely enough, to kill them, before sudden death intervenes, or the false appearance of good-liking gives place to emaciation. The penalty, which is to follow, for departing from the organic law, is not thought of; though it is matter of common observation, that the flesh of wild animals, which live after nature's intention, is of much easier digestion than that of our domestic cattle—an observation, which might have led sooner to the inquiry, what injuries we are bringing on ourselves, through the vicious manner in which we are treating them.

The prohibition of fat almost includes that of swine's flesh. A further reason might be found in the animal's filthy habits of feeding. Fed as these creatures generally are among us, on animal and vegetable substances in a state of incipient putrefaction, their flesh must be any thing but wholesome, and, I believe, is a fruitful source of scrofula, and other diseases. In warmer climates the consequences must be still worse, as in leprosy, of which, I believe, it is the most common cause.

The great amount of holy-day season, enjoined on the Israelites through Moses, doubtless seems to be a great drawback on the great business of life, to those political economists, who (in the language of Combe) " appear to conceive man's chief end, in Britain at least, to be to manufacture hard-ware, broad-cloths, and cotton goods for the use of the whole world, and to store up wealth." * But the multiplication of

* Lectures on Popular Education, p. 69.

holy-day seasons tended to save the Israelites from the very evil, which Combe so deeply laments in his countrymen—"the excessive cultivation of Acquisitiveness." It tended to secure the good, which this philosopher and his associates are aiming at, in urging the necessity of gradually reducing the time of work for the laboring classes to about eight hours per day; that they may have sufficient time for intellectual and moral improvement, that the whole man may be duly cultivated. At a time when books were scarce, and lyceums and lectureships not the order of the day, the assembling of the whole country three times a year at the great festivals, afforded substantially the advantage of these modern improvements: it afforded opportunity to compare ideas with men of other provinces, and to improve by an interchange of knowledge. How different must the populace of such a country have been, from the tasked and confined operatives and peasantry of Europe!

Again, it was enjoined in the Mosaic institutions, that the land should rest every seventh year. In addition to what has just been stated, I venture to say, after paying not a very little attention to agriculture both theoretically and

practically, that land ought to rest this proportion of time : that by forcing a crop each year
through a long series, we exhaust and disease
the soil : the produce on the whole is less, and
becomes ill-fitted for food of man or beast.
During the fallow year, time might have been
taken to free the land from various noxious
weeds. Or it might have been trenched, in
order to bring uppermost a new portion of the
soil for cultivation the coming six years : and
there is some testimony to prove, that such was
actually the practice of the Jews.

I can select only a few specimens bearing
upon the point in question. I have a strong
suspicion, that a thorough examination of the
subject would satisfy every fair inquirer, that
Moses could have so well anticipated views, to
which the most practical inquirers of this late
age are coming, only through divine inspiration.
He did not prescribe morality and religion alone.
He knew that it was in vain to look for manly
piety, honorable to God, among a people who
neglected to observe in due proportion the
physical and organic, as well as the moral laws.
He encouraged the cultivation of intellect, and
of the social affections. In reward for observing
his statutes, God promised to bless their bread

and their water, and to take sickness away from the midst of them. (Ex. xxiii. 25.) There is no need of supposing, this was to be done by any extraordinary providence : we may consider it as the natural result of due attention to cleanliness, proper cultivation of the soil, judiciously interchanging labor with recreation and cultivation of the intellectual and moral faculties; of not pursuing wealth as life's whole aim and end; of being temperate in all things. I intend to pursue further the thoughts now suggested.

BODY AND SOUL.

No. II.

WE boast of the improvements of the age—of the excellence of our civil and domestic institutions. Let us just consider some particulars, in which we profess to have improved on the wisdom of former ages.

Our agriculturalists exact of the soil an annual return. It is in·vain, that God has so constituted it as to require septennially or thereabouts a year of rest. Acquisitiveness will not be so restrained. Artificial manuring must supply what God intended should be effected by other means. Mark the cattle feeding. How luxuriant and beautiful to the eye is the herbage, where their manure is dropped. But the animals avoid it, and crop again and again the scanty grass which intervenes. Instinct teaches them, that the grass so fair to the eye is bad for the stomach. But man goes right counter to the important lesson thus taught him. He covers his whole field with a top-dressing of rank manure; and compels his cattle to eat the grass and hay thus grown, or starve. His milch cows escape with comparative impunity: for nature has provided, that noxious particles taken in the food shall be secreted by the milk-vessels: and the heaviest part of the penalty falls on those, who feed on the milk, or on the butter and cheese manufactured out of it.

I venture to affirm, that around our cities especially, by far the largest part of the land is diseased by forced cropping, over manuring, and noxious weeds. But it would require a volume to treat of bad husbandry as a source of disease. Perhaps we should trace the evil back to the ceasing to yield to agriculture that pre-eminence among the arts, which God indicated in appointing Adam to till the ground, and in constituting his chosen people so eminently an agricultural people. Now, if one son in the family is supposed to give indications of superior parts, it is thought a pity to •retain him on the farm; he is sent to the counting-room; and it seems to me, as if the conscious earth resented the indignity. We may expect wiser conduct, when it shall be better understood, how much agriculture requires to be reformed by the light of science truly so called.

Again, the wisdom of the world thinks to have relieved itself of a great burden, in throwing off the impositions of priestcraft. So indignantly does it resent the waste of time spent for honoring the Lord, that it will not yield him one day in seven. In most parts of our country, stages and steam-boats make no distinction between the days of the week; and worldly business and recreations are as rife on the Lord's day, as on others.

So in fancied freedom, men smile at the tithed dupes of other days, and at those who voluntarily tax themselves for the support of the gospel. A scanty portion of the support allotted to the Levites is allowed even to the teachers of literature and science. Let us just glance at the evils we are suffering for departing so widely from the spirit of the social institutions, which God once granted to his people.

The average duration of human life among the Israelites, seems to have been reckoned at about seventy years : (Ps. xc. 10.)· With us it is only about half that sum, or something less. Their diseases were few and simple ; such as hardly required a distinct profession for their cure. With us they have been multiplied and aggravated with fearful rapidity ; notwithstanding the expense of money and talent, at which about a third part of our educated men are set apart to study their origin and remedies. They who land on our shores from foreign countries, speak with surprise of the sickly forms, which every where meet them, so different from the healthy countenances common in Europe. I am told, that Dr. Jackson, in a recent public lecture to the citizens of Boston, adverted to this fact in proof of the bad quality of the water of our cities. But I believe, that " water " is only one article among many, in which we have forfeited the divine blessing, by being wise in our own conceits. (Ex. xxiii. 25.) The superiority of the German students to our own, in uniting intense study with vigorous health, is well known.

Again, the mortality among our young children vastly exceeds what takes place among the young of any of the more perfectly organized animals. They have instinct alone for their guide; and following it simply, fulfil the end of their being. It is derogatory to the divine good ness, to suppose, that man may not generally fill the number of his days indicated by his organization, as well as the inferior animals. But man, in addition to instinct, has for guides, reason, experience, the word of God. These teach him, that he was created for nobler ends, than to lay up wealth, as life's supreme good. If he will not listen to the admonition, he must suffer loss in the very good at which he so eagerly grasps.

A case now in my eye, though an extreme one, still represents too justly the case of our country at large. A farmer cultivated his farm like one resolved to make the most of it. He was esteemed as a thrifty man. Besides a fine stock of cattle, he had money to some considerable amount, accumulated by his own industry, at interest. But he had no thoughts for the other world, or even for the more ennobling concerns of this. His Sabbaths were spent in looking after the business of his farm. He has now been for several years the tenant of a retreat for the insane. I have no doubt, that his insanity was contracted by his unbending concentration of thought upon one grovelling pursuit : and that, had his Sabbaths been devoted to Him who claims them as his own, and had the instruction of his children and the operations of evangelical benevolence duly entered into his every day calculations, he might now have been in the full enjoyment of all his powers.

BODY AND SOUL.

No. III.

Sana mens in corpore sano.

IF there was in the institutions of Moses a divine wisdom, which aimed at a sound body as essentially requisite in order to the sound mind, we need not go far to find a sufficient reason for some obvious defects in the religious character of our age, and especially of our country. Obscurely as truths were revealed under the ancient dispensation, there appears an evenness and a completeness in the character of the Old Testament saints, for which at the present day we might long seek in vain.* Among Christians, what sectarian rancor do we witness! what irritability of temper! what transient heats and long languors in religious zeal! The remedies most urgently recommended are, intenser prayer, stricter keeping of the heart, more self-distrust, greater activity in the service of God and men's souls, and others of like character. All these things ought to be done: but while some other things are left quite undone, I have no expectation of seeing the end attained. I hold, that the bodies of Christians have become so unfit residences of the Holy Spirit, that we need seek no stronger reason, why his influences are so feeble and variable there—so hardly distinguishable from animal heats and irregularities.

It is eminently a time, when we may complain, "O the hope of Israel, the Saviour thereof in time of trouble, why shouldest thou be as a stranger in the land, and as a wayfaring man

---

* If there is any thing in the church at this time in which there is a greater deficiency than in any other, it is this, that there is so little completeness of Christian character.—*Memoir of Anna Jane Linnard, p.* 87.

that turneth aside to tarry for a night? Why shouldest thou be as a man astonied, as a mighty man that cannot save?"—Jer. xiv. 8, 9. It is pretty evident, that the means hitherto chiefly relied on for sustaining religion in the church, are losing their efficacy. Protracted meetings, and the kindred system of operations, have served their turn and done good. True, their enemies have objected, that religion was represented as a periodical or occasional thing, rather than as a steadily governing principle. I hold the objection about as reasonable, as to maintain, that a dead body is better than a living one, the latter being subject to feverish heats and convulsive throes. Still, we should not rest content with entertaining the Saviour " as a stranger in the land, and as a wayfaring man that turneth aside to tarry for a night." And he now seems warning us to prepare for his steady abiding with us, or to calculate on his utter withdrawal. Now I firmly believe, that the point, to which the attention of Christians needs most particularly to be directed, is the study of the elements of physiology, and the influence of the body on the mind. I expect only a puny, inefficient, inconstant race of Christians, where the soil is cultivated so little on scientific principles, and such food is eaten as such a soil produces. Few seem to trace intemperate sallies of passion, blunted senses which require to be taught once and again the first principles of the oracles of God, feverish contentions about hair-breadth varieties of opinion or mere verbal differences, to a physical cause. Few, I believe, justly estimate, how much may be traced to stomachs long irritated by ill-digestible materials, where, to keep down acid fermentations, resort has long been had to tea, coffee, tobacco, brandy, opium, cayenne or hot drops, according to the individual's fancy.

Much has been said of ardent spirit as the great source of vice and misery: and I believe, it has not been condemned too utterly. At the same time, to banish alcohol entirely, both in the form of distilled and fermented liquors, and there stop, I should consider an achievement about as important, as to dip a bucket of water out of Charles river, when our object was to dry up the stream. It is not the single article that is working so much mischief; it is a thousand. Let any one judge for himself, after feeding awhile on the sponge-balls sold from our bakeries; or after looking into some of the total abstinence families who have lived several years on the produce of some of our farms, which have been well forced into good liking by the rank materials carted out from the city, and not well tempered with lime, or other corrective. I fully believe, that much of the milk so produced for the market, is a more pernicious beverage than pure brandy and water. But perhaps it is unfair to specify any instances, when there are so many, too numerous to mention, equally deserving.

As things are, the temperance cause labors under a vast disadvantage. Indeed, I know, that some of its earliest and warmest friends, men too of curious observation, have lately expressed the opinion, that in some of our cities the total abstinence men suffer more than the moderate drinkers. I can easily believe the fact possible. I can easily believe that the removal of one item from such a frightful round of unsuspected evils, would produce disarrangement and dissension, worse, apparently (at least) than the forced quiet kept up before; even if this should not be restored by worse means than that for which they were substituted.

By the researches of the wise men of this world, God is again revealing with fresh light the truth so constantly implied in ancient revelation, that body and soul are intimately united, and that it is in vain to expect one worthily to reflect the image of its Maker, while the cultivation of the other is sadly neglected. The church must no longer neglect a truth so important. This neglect has already cost her the loss of too many of her brightest ornaments and ablest defenders in the midst of their usefulness. It is vain under such loss to talk of the mysteries of Providence. There is no mystery about the matter, except so far as it is mysterious how the infatuation of men takes place under the providence of God. The plain truth is, (enough for us to know,) through careless ignorance or wilful obstinacy, we have been living in flagrant violation of laws open to our investigation in the works of nature, and not obscurely intimated (many of them) in the word of God; and we have only suffered the penalty consequent on such transgression. We have talked enough of the depressed state of religion, the increase of vice, error and infidelity, the activity of the agents of darkness, and the need of God's interposing Spirit. I hope the heart-searchings and the prayers of the closet have corresponded. If so, then I expect also to see Christians generally making it a matter of conscience to inquire, how they shall render their bodies more fit temples for the Holy Spirit's residence; to make an effort to provide themselves with plain and wholesome food; and to encounter the self-denial of bringing stomachs accustomed to a most vicious mode of living to crave no other stimulus. I forbear to enter into detail on these and kindred points; because my end is better answered, if the reader is sufficiently convinced of the importance of the views I have suggested, to subscribe for the Moral Reformer, a work too cheap, too good in its design (as I am confident it will be in its execution) to be a stranger in any Christian family.

BODY AND SOUL.

No. IV.

I HAVE before remarked, how an acknowledgment of the intimate connection between body and soul—of the necessity of thoroughly cultivating each in order to the perfection of the other—pervades the Mosaic institutions. After

3 *

long neglect, the principle is again attracting the attention of thinking men. Like all new thoughts especially, it is liable to be extravagantly and erroneously applied. A sound mind, in the apostolic sense, is eminently needed here. I hope, it is not anti-spiritual to say, that the sound mind is so hardly to be expected apart from the sound body, that we may well suspect the judgment of those, who think to set off the celestial genius of their idol, by contrasting it with its feeble, trembling bodily frame. I fear, we shall too generally find in such geniuses, a few prominent sparkling traits of mind, with a sad want of harmonious balance between its powers.

I hail the progress of phrenology, so far at least as recognizing the principle in question; and this without at all committing myself to maintain, that the science is as sure or as practical, as its decided votaries profess. I find no objection to its truth in the fact, that the acknowledged leaders of the public mind have generally been disposed to treat it with ridicule and contempt. If it be really founded in truth, and more than a very little in advance of thoughts previously admitted, nothing else was to be expected, judging from all past history. The fame of Columbus and Galileo is purchased at the cost of first being treated as a madman or driveler.

If the truth of phrenology should come to be generally acknowledged, no doubt, it will share the fate of astronomy and geology, in being pressed into the service of irreligion : nor need we doubt, that the attempt will again be worse than a failure. Indeed while yet to illustrate religion by the light of phrenology has hardly been thought of, its truth being admitted seems to afford one of the best vindications of two of the doctrines, which the wisdom of the world has most labored to philosophize out of the Bible. First, it entirely overturns the Arminian notions of moral agency, as if this implied contingency, absence of bias, a self-determining power of the will—as if the voluntary acts of free agents could not be calculated on with moral certainty. Again, phrenology falls in completely with what seems to be implied in the apostle's reasoning, 1 Cor. xv., as well as other Scriptures ; namely, that man was originally created body and soul, each being essential to perfect man ; that "immortality was the condition of creation, and death came in as a surprise upon nature;"* and that the redemption of

---

* Sherlock.

Christ is not perfect, till man be restored to immortality of both body and soul. I shall in this number use the language of phrenology. It will save circumlocution, and render the sense plainer and more satisfactory to one class of readers: while they who recognize only the general principle of the sound mind and the sound body contributing each to either, will be able, I hope, to change the language, and find no substantial fault of argument.

Nothing seems at present better established, than that religion thrives best left to its own energies, unhampered by the professed protection of state establishments. A plausible objection may hence be derived against the ecclesiastical constitution of the Hebrews. But we are hardly driven to the necessity of maintaining, that God committed the superintendence of religion among them to a privileged order, purposely to show, by preserving a goodly religious influence through a series of ages, that there was a superior unseen power at work, reversing the results, which have uniformly come forth, wherever human wisdom has committed a general interest to the like keeping. As with other general interests, so with religion, there seems to be a stage in the progress of society, before which, purely republican principles do not succeed; and after which, aristocracy and monopoly invariably work the like ill effects.

Now, if man is furnished with an organ of Veneration, to be cultivated in common and in harmony with others; before spiritual views of God come to be generally and strongly apprehended, other means for the exercise of veneration seem requisite. Philosophers, nay, Christian doctors, have accordingly justified the imposition of image-worship on the populace. With more wisdom, God, as a temporary expedient, and during the early development of human thought, established a splendid ritual, and holy priesthood. So too, in detesting the impositions almost every where practised on the multitude by the splendor of royalty and nobility, we ought not to overlook the consideration, that where God is not spiritually apprehended, the welfare of man requires some object for the exercise of his Veneration: and so far at least, these pageants may serve a good purpose.

Here comes in a consideration peculiarly interesting to our countrymen. From among us the habit of venerating an institution for its antiquity or unknown origin, or an order of men as invested with some mysterious science or divine right, has entirely disappeared; unless some shreds of it still hang around medical science : and these are fast disappearing before the inquiring spirit of the age, which is hastening to the conclusion, that the essential principles, on which health depends, are few and intelligible to the mind generally enlightened; and that so far as cures are wrought by medical skill beyond the patient's comprehension, the physician was not very wide from the truth, who defined his art to be " the art of amusing the patient till nature works a cure." It is said, that the heads of Americans generally exhibit the organ of Veneration less than in almost any other people. Now, if the mental faculty is really connected, as here supposed, with physical organization, its disuse must tend directly to the deterioration of the whole physical frame, since, for the perfection of each part, every other must be duly exercised. Here may be one cause of our physical ills adverted to in a former number. And here too we see in a new light why, all inferior objects of veneration having lost their power, we need especially the power of genuine religion to save us both body and soul.

There is apparently at least a great difficulty

in reconciling peace principles, as often taught,
with the divine commission given to the Israelites
to exterminate the nations of Canaan. Let us
try to hope for the universal reign of peace and
pacific principles, without leaving a shadow of
suspicion on any thing which God has enjoined.
If Combativeness and Destructiveness are essential parts of the human constitution, they too
should be exercised in their own turn and proportion. They had been restrained by the
bondage in Egypt. It might have been necessary to call them into exercise, to give edge to
the mind, and decision to the character of the
people; controlling their exercise at the same
time by Conscientiousness and Benevolence.
Accordingly, though commissioned to combat
and destroy, they were expressly informed, that
they were used as instruments in the hands of a
just God to exterminate the devoted nations for
their abominable iniquities; and warned, that
themselves should suffer the like, if they fell into
the like practices; while a promise was given,
that in the seed planted in the place of the ex-
tirpated race, all the nations of the earth should
be blessed.

At the period of the reformation, the world
was in a state to afford exercise to Combative-

ness and Destructiveness in another and nobler way, than through feats of physical courage. There were enormities of doctrine and abuses of practice to be assailed and overcome by argument and ridicule. Combativeness and Destructiveness were called into action together with the intellectual and moral faculties. The result was an awakening of thought—a development of intellectual vigor—such as the world had not witnessed before.

If there is any justness in the views now presented, the true way to establish universal and perpetual peace, is not to deny the legitimacy of the faculties, which war calls into exercise, but to provide for their activity in a way more accordant with the improved condition of the world. The work of reform is not completed. Errors still swarm, which need to be refuted. There are still faults abundant in our systems of education, and in our social institutions, which require a master's correction, or we should not be so far behind the ancient people of God, in physical vigor, and in completeness of religious character. To search out and put down the immediate and remote causes of evils so obvious and so oppressive, will afford ample range for all lawful gratification of the propensities to combat and to destroy, while love to God and good-will towards man shall be more vigorous, for the harmony with which faculties so often set in opposition, can now act together.

BODY AND SOUL.

No. V.

I DO not think that a thorough physical education would require of students a very great proportion of time for bodily exercise. On the contrary, I believe that a good acquaintance with the various agents affecting our health, and a practical regard to the corresponding laws, would save many hours spent in bodily exercise, required not by the necessity of our constitution, but as the penalty of infringing its laws in the misuse of the stomach, brain, skin, and other organs. I believe that the German students secure their better health with less time spent in exercise, than ours generally employ. I might urge then the importance of physical education on the very ground of redeeming more time for intellectual pursuits; though I can hardly give him credit for the art of thinking, who has never found his best intellectual efforts to have been made on days, when ten or twelve hours were spent in bodily labor, and an hour employed in the evening to put into form the result of the day's thoughts.

In making education practical, there is no need of dispensing with intense or abstract thinking—no need of vindicating the thought-saving scheme, on which it has become so fashionable to compose school books. We need not rob Greek, Latin and Mathematics of their due importance, in requiring that into our systems of education should enter some instruction of the young into the constitution of their own bodies, and the agents affecting them. It is shameful to fill the heads of youth with the knowledge *of names*, perhaps in half a dozen different languages, while they are left profoundly ignorant of almost all the *things* around them. A large majority probably of those among us who are supposed to have received a finished education, know how to distinguish some five or six of the most common rocks; about twice that number of our common birds; know as much of the properties of plants, as suffices not to substitute ivy or henbane for any of the garden esculents ; and as little of the Linnæan system of classification as they do of the geography of Saturn ; while their knowledge of other things corresponds. Or, if this is an account of what has been, rather than what is, the change is quite recent, and very imperfectly effected.

A system of education claiming the name of liberal, ought to embrace such instruction in the elements of physiology, in the Materia Medica too, especially the botanic department, as to qualify each to practice *la plus salutaire des medecines, celle qui s' attache plus a prevenir les maux qu' a les guerir;* and even to know how to exercise some discrimination on emergencies, when professional advice cannot be seasonably called. The knowledge I would recommend, tends neither to undervalue more profound professional skill, nor to dispense with the necessity of professional advisers ; any more than the Protestant doctrine of the right of private judgment supersedes the necessity of extraordinary biblical research, or of the Christian ministry. But it is desirable that every one should be able to decide, when to call in medical advice is necessary, and then to listen to it like a rational being. The liberal-minded

and benevolent physician would feel a satisfaction in administering to such patients, superior
to that of being blindly reverenced for the exer
cise of some mysterious, incomprehensible art ;
as the evangelical pastor finds a purer pleasure
in enlightening and guiding souls inquiring the
way of salvation, than the Romish priest can
know in exacting a surrender of reason and
conscience, from the dupes, who, content with
the *opus operatum*, have no general principles
for their direction in cases where specific directions from their superior are wanting. Protestants as we boast to be, there is too much popery
among us, in regard to the body at least. Let
us aim to be Protestants in regard to this also.
I mean, as we expect every Christian to have
an enlightened conscience for a sufficient guide
in all ordinary circumstances, and to have his
understanding in difficulties enlightened, not
dictated to, by his pastor ; as we expect him to
exercise repentance as a free, intelligible act,
and not to do a penance, for which he can give
no more rational account than that Father Con-
fessor so prescribes ; so, unless the body with its
functions is more difficult to comprehend than
the soul, let us aim to make such instruction
general, that men shall not continually err

grossly in diet and regimen, or be at a nonplus under every little ailment ; that on the great and rare occasions when that knowledge which few can possess is really necessary, they may not submit to it so blindly, that the result is pretty sure to be life or death, as Veneration and Hope, or as Cautiousness is most active.

I know that good books and good professors are extremely scarce for the instruction I am recommending ; just because public sentiment has been so silent as to demanding any thing of the kind. Let its tone change, and the *desideratum* will soon be supplied. Our Saviour acted on the principle of doing good to the bodies of men, to win the way for advice as to their souls. Though miracles have ceased, there is a vast field for inquiry into the art of preserving health, so unoccupied, nor yet requiring very much time for coming to some satisfactory results, that a new generation of ministers may fairly resolve on qualifying themselves for rendering such advice to their people, as, for preparing the way for religious instruction, and as a pledge of seeking their good,—shall be next to the power of working miracles.

AN APPEAL

TO THE MEMBERS OF THE THREE LEARNED PROFESSIONS.

IT is in vain to attempt concealing that there
is at work a spirit of ultraism, radicalism, anti-
ism, and infidelity, which is aiming to bring
your professions into discredit, as the threefold
band which binds in slavery the human mind,
and stays the progress of general improvement.
Men so affected argue thus : The legal profession, by its education and constitution, is made
to flourish best in a quarrelsome community.
Legislation very much, and jurisprudence altogether, fall into the hands of men, whose
interest it is to render law complicated and
obscure, and entangle people in difficulties.
The medical profession likewise is not constituted to teach people the art of preserving
health, but to take advantage of the errors committed through ignorance of such art. And
though the Reformation did away the former

constitution, by which the priests were made inevitably to " eat up the sin of the people, and set their heart on their iniquity," [connive at the vices, which were filling their own coffers,] yet the men, whose mode of arguing we are reviewing, choose to overlook this fact, and fix attention rather on another, namely, that the three professions are educated at the same colleges, and are apparently firmly united in maintaining each other's acknowledged rights. Hence the indiscriminate assault upon the whole.

Now whatever qualifying considerations men of discrimination may oppose to the sweeping conclusion, we can hardly show, that there is not truth enough in the reasoning, to render it a powerful engine with a people so restlessly inquisitive, so given to change, as ours. I would propose the means of averting the calamity which threatens. My proposal is briefly this, not to await the outbreaking of the tempest, but now, while you can do it with credit, to give your hearty concurrence to doing away the constitution of things, on which the objections are raised, and introducing such a change, that people shall pay for knowledge, rather than be taxed for ignorance.

I will give a specimen of the evils requiring

correction. It was lately asked of a lawyer in one of the principal manufacturing towns of New England, how many of his profession would be wanted in his town, if they acted on evangelical principles? ("Blessed are the peacemakers.") He answered *five*. The existing number is about twenty-five. What a waste of talent, just because we do not make it the interest of our lawyers to be peacemakers! while we are daily assailed with the cry of the want of educated teachers at the West.

I will give an instance of what I mean by having people pay for knowledge, rather than be taxed for ignorance. Suppose the city of Boston should employ two physicians (more if necessary) to each Ward, to be paid competent salaries for administering to all the sickness, more or less, within their respective Wards, with one general superintendent. These would keep their eyes wide open, to watch for disease in its causes. They would watch the bakers, whether they were using bad flour, or mixing pernicious articles with their bread. They would watch the market in all its departments. They would lecture people publicly on the means of preserving health. They would be instant in season and out of season, to enforce these means. Thus nine-tenths of the existing sickness would be prevented. For it is acknowledged, that thus much of our diseases, at least, arises from violating the laws of our being; and people could much better pay the same sum for instruction in these laws, than as a penalty for their violation.

Such a change would be the best of all defences against quackery. We have tried what legislation, and argument, and ridicule could do, under the present constitution of things. But so easy is it in this country to throw odium upon whatever looks like monopoly, chartered rights, and exclusive privileges, that the very force, which has been arrayed in defence of the regular practice, bids fair to recoil on the same with destructive force, for its anti-republican aspect. Let scientific physicians concur to bring about such a change, that people shall pay for health, and not for sickness—let them thus do away all cause for suspicion, that they are jealous of real improvements in medicine, and there will remain little cause of complaint, that men of influence countenance unscientific pretenders.

There is one aspect of the community, which seems to me to demand the serious consideration of medical practitioners, and those looking forward to the profession. In regard to temperance, society is separating into two divisions. On the one hand are those, who mean to carry out the principle of being temperate in all things; who consider, that God in his word has repeatedly promised health and long life as the rewards of keeping the whole of his law; who are making it a matter of conscience to inquire, how we have violated, his law, moral or physiological, that the average number of our days is only about half that granted to the ancient Israelites; who will not be satisfied, till they have discovered the error and corrected it. On the other hand is the reckless portion of the community, who mean to give the reins to appetite; and when the constitution runs down, wish to wind it up, as quick as possible, and give the reins to appetite again. This class are fast falling into the Thomsonian practice, as the best of any thing for their purpose. Neither of these classes affords much encouragement to those, who are anticipating to practice medicine according to the present system. That this state of things is so little regarded at the fountain heads of lore and wisdom, I can only resolve into the general fact, that they have ever been the last practically to regard changes well understood every where else. But it really seems to me, as if our medical professors were acting very much like the hen, when she hides her head, and seems to think herself secure from danger.

Let a beginning be made (as I have instanced above) of substituting the purchase of knowledge for the tax of ignorance, and its advantages would soon become so apparent as best for all concerned, that I think the principle would soon be carried into every department, where it is yet wanted. It would so increase the love of knowledge, and the means of purchasing it, as to increase, I verily believe, the encouragement held out to thoroughly educated men.

I cannot now go into the details of the plan I propose; but I think I have sufficiently explained its fundamental principles. Some may be disposed to smile at it, as a pleasing but impracticable speculation. Let such reflect how rapidly in these times public sentiment has been revolutionized on many points. Let them reflect again, that so changeable are all things now, that which was in repute yesterday being an abomination to-day, that he who regards but his own comfort, has small inducement to trim his sails to the popular gale, but seems cast by Divine Providence on a sort of necessity, to take his stand firmly on what he honestly believes to be truth and right, and leave the world to come into his views at its leisure (rather in its haste.) Let the clergy especially consider, that they have already been so well sifted, (not thoroughly, I confess,) that the independent course now exacted of them need cost very little indeed.

One word more. The change now proposed, by making it the interest of lawyers to keep people peaceable, and of physicians to keep them healthy, would not only promote their own quiet by screening them from jealousy, but would render them very acute for their own interest to discern, what system of religious teaching best renders people orderly and temperate ; and they would throw their influence accordingly. And now, good reader, do you not see that all this would be just so much clear gain to your own denomination ? I expect, therefore, that you at least will consider of my proposal, and favor its adoption.

A SECOND APPEAL

TO THE THREE LEARNED PROFESSIONS.

A FEW weeks since the writer took the liberty to address a Circular to the presidents of most of the New England colleges, expressing views kindred to those of his last Appeal, but in a manner, which seemed to him more proper for private suggestion, than for publication at present. He complained that our social institutions and our systems of education, were based on a practical denial of some truths, admitted by most Christians to be fundamental principles of revelation ; and urged the necessity of an immediate effort for some changes, going to a depth, which some might stigmatize as *radicalism*. He is happy to acknowledge the receipt of an answer from the president of one of our colleges, (second to none for furnishing thorough scholars and practical men,) acknowledging the necessity of applying *radicalism* (in its legitimate meaning)

at all the sources of moral influence, more in-
dustriously than the times have yet permitted:
declaring the increasing interest, with which he
had long revolved the subjects suggested in the
Circular ; and the harmonious concurrence of
the Corporation and Faculty, with which he is
associated, to correct the glaring discrepance
existing between the Christianity professed in
our colleges and the mode in which education
has been there conducted ; of which correction
he gives a good account of the beginning there
made. I cannot doubt, that the change there
begun, will so manifest its advantages in furnishing superior men for every exigency, that our
other colleges must follow the example, or be
left "like hulks anchored in the stream of time,
serving to show how fast the current of general
improvement is passing by." *

---

* I have no intent of representing this comparison as
really applicable to our colleges in their present state ;
still I cannot but agree with many of the best friends of
education, that there is no necessity, why, after one has
completed what is nominally his education, his real education should be hardly begun. The managers of our
colleges and professional schools need to be reminded,
that the world is fast discovering the evils incident to
the possession of funds, to the habit of going in a prescribed track, and to being venerated as wisdom's and

The writer several years since engaged some-what zealously in inculcating some sentiments, which sounded new to most ears, the leading principles of which were, that to carry forward reform and improvement, we ought to abolish all monopolies * and mysteries, make the interest and duty of every class of men coincide, and have people pay for knowledge rather than be taxed for ignorance. In urging the immediate, full, and practical admission of these principles

---

learning's highest seats. The only remedy I would now propose for these evils is, the encouragement of other seminaries founded on a juster estimate of human nature and the wants of the American people ; and that private or *self*-education be more duly appreciated. I would not discredit our theological seminaries. They certainly possess some advantages over the old way of studying with a parish minister; while this also has its advantages for introducing the student into the practical duties of his profession. I would have a class educated both ways, that by comparison, each might learn better its own defects, and be excited to a holy emulation.

* A great step towards perfection, would be the full and practical admission of the principle, that every one has the right to employ his talents to the utmost for his own benefit, as far as he can do it without injuring others. This system of government is certainly far su-perior to that of exclusive privileges of any kind. * * * Monopoly impedes improvement in every thing.—Spurz-heim on Education, pp. 182, 190.

as the great *desideratum* for giving an impulse onward to the human mind, like that created by the Reformation, though at the cost of being pitied as a fanatic, a visionary, and a dreamy speculator, he was conscious of being entitled to no peculiar credit for independence : so fully was he satisfied, that by the mutation of these times, Divine Providence was casting us on a sort of necessity to take our stand firmly on what we honestly believe to be truth and right, and let the world give in its accordance, when it is ready : so clearly did he see, that this restlessly inquiring and novel-seeking age must before long pay some attention to his principles ; and so sure was he, that once firmly grasped, their truth and importance would be so fully felt, that they never would be abandoned. He is now happy to acknowledge the testimonials coming in from all quarters, and from men generally acknowledged as of sound judgment, giving in their accordance with the writer's views. Thus with confirmed confidence, he invites all, by the manifest folly of steering by a breath so changeable as the popular gale, to inquire freely, and decide firmly.

I believe I have never written or uttered any thing, and hope I never shall write or utter any thing, in regard to my favorite views, to require a formal protestation, that, as I know my own heart, I am not actuated by anger or hatred towards any class of men. I am confident, that they who are familiar with my writings and conversation, will not suspect me of being otherwise actuated, than by a desire to promote the best temporal and eternal welfare of the members of each of the three learned professions, as well as of society at large. And if any should undertake the defence of my principles by writing or orally, I hope they will take care, not only so to feel, but so to express themselves, as never to be suspected of feeling otherwise. Especially I pray, that these principles may never be made hobbies for party organization. I honestly think them too pure and respectable for such prostitution.

One very much neglected principle of Christianity and of sound philosophy is, that "He who is not for me is against me;" or, that whoever loves not his neighbor as himself—has not an ardent desire, like Howard, to promote the welfare of mankind—a decided determination for this end to sacrifice ease and interest, professional pride and whatever else—he is fairly construed as an enemy of his species; and will manifest himself as decidedly such, when placed in circumstances of open conflict between his interest and theirs. (Comp. Rom. vii. 7—13, viii. 7.) Equally clear is it, that such philanthropy is comparatively rare among men; and very peculiarly must that body of men be constituted, in which it is the ruling principle. Of course whatever body is not so peculiarly constituted, is constructively at enmity with the welfare of mankind in such a sense, that it will be sure to sacrifice that welfare to its **own** present interest, when they come into conflict. This simple principle, and this only, fully explains, why aristocracies, monopolies, and mysterles, have so completely contradicted in fact all that their friends have theorized in their favor; and why the wisdom of this world has so often reasoned so sadly amiss, when it seemed only to be taking hold of the certain advantages of the division of labor.

That the wise of this world have not more fully attended in practice to the curse pronounced on him that trusteth in man, (Jer. xvii. 5.) has arisen, I think, from a desire to evade the corresponding charge of deceit and wickedness, (v. 9.) and to find generally prevalent a powerful counteracting force of humane feeling and sense of honor. Vain effort! we may **say,** without adopting the peculiarities of any sect. So have said men the most diverse in their sectarian theology. Says Spurzheim,* "The members of the ordinary professions do not think it necessary to conceal, that the end and aim of all their exertions is selfishness." Says the Rev. Mr. Walker, "I fear, we have been a little too eloquent in our praises of human virtue : I believe, that generally and practically speaking, men are just as good as they are required to be by public opinion, and no better." †

I have spoken of the evils which seem to threaten your professions more or less from the revolutionary character of the age. My best advice is, as God has promised all other things to them who seek first the kingdom of heaven, take him at his word. Resolve in good earnest to seek above all things the advancement of his kingdom, by doing away, as your education and talents have fitted you, the evils, which hinder men from reflecting clearly in body and soul the image of their Maker. You may then fairly expect him to add all things necessary for this life, as a pledge of the safety of trusting his word for the life which is to come.

---

* On Education, p. 271.

† Election Sermon, (quoted from memory.)

A THIRD APPEAL

TO THE THREE LEARNED PROFESSIONS.

Suppose the ancient legislators of this Commonwealth had incorporated a company of merchants with the exclusive privilege of dealing in merchandize, to admit whom they pleased into their own number, to enact their own by-laws and fix their own prices. Suppose the people had been persuaded that this was all right and proper, and that they were deeply indebted to these merchants for furnishing them with the means of living. We can easily imagine, how much might have been argued in favor of such a course. It might have been defended as necessary to maintain the respectability of the mercantile profession; to protect the public from the impositions of incompetent and knavish traders. We might have been told of the long apprenticeship necessary to instruct one in all the mysteries of trade; and of the advantages of a regularly organized body, to check the circulation of pernicious articles : especially the inducement they would have from self-interest, to check such a free use of ardent spirits, as would render thousands unable to pay their debts, or provide their families with the necessaries of life. But after all that might have been thus reasoned, I believe we shall pretty well agree, that the evidence of experience would have fully refuted the reasoning—that the scheme would have produced far worse evils than those arising from the present free competition, and the excessive spirit of speculation.

Let us suppose moreover the above imagined scheme to be an anomaly in our social institutions, monopolies and exclusive pretensions to be generally odious, the people to be as now restlessly inquisitive, and jealous of their republican rights. Suppose they have tolerated the anti-republican anomaly some centuries, because their attention has not been directed towards it; because they have been so busily engaged in fighting the cause of freedom, and establishing republican principles in other departments; because they have been so proud of their achievements in the cause of liberty and independence, that He " whose service is perfect freedom," has justly permitted the delusion, to reserve its exposure to be brought out for the mortification of their pride, whenever he sees fit. Suppose again, that in the natural progress of free inquiry, attention begins to be excited towards the anti-republican anomaly; hints are thrown out pretty freely, that from the general selfishness of mankind, and the known tendency of privileged bodies to be very barren of fruits for the public good, it would be strange indeed, if behind the veil a good deal of imposition were not practised on popular credulity. Now, from the habit of resting on their privileges, and the implicit deference of the community, would not the incorporated merchants be in great danger of not anticipating the change in public sentiment seasonably enough, to yield their antiquated pretensions with such good grace as to save their credit with the public? Would not he who warned them so to do, very probably be treated with contempt, or as an impertinent troubler of undisputed rights? By a little excess of obstinacy in not yielding to the changes of the times, would they not run the risk of being overwhelmed at last by an undeserved torrent of public contempt or public indignation? In short, would they not be in imminent hazard of incurring a fate like that of Charles and of Louis in political life, who, for not yielding a little to the popular current in season, found at last all concessions vain, and were plunged ten thousand fathoms beneath the flood?

As I write for men accustomed to compare and infer, I do not think it necessary to detail where, and how nearly may be found parallels to the supposition above made. I think something more or less like it might be found in more than one or two departments.

If your three professions were fully based upon those principles of human nature, which Christianity and republicanism teach, (and in my view they closely harmonize,) I think we should be rid of some such evils as the following. Attention would be less directed towards vice and wretchedness in their specific forms, and more to the root and principle. We should be spared the abundance of disgusting details laid before the public of the abuses of the reproductive function, and see more effort made to resist the pernicious and expensive fashions, which render it so hard for young men to enter the domestic relation, and to correct the errors of diet, which unnaturally stimulate the appetites. We should not have one editor denouncing the distilleries, and another the confectioners' shops, as almost the only fountain-heads of vice, poverty and disease. We should not have a party with their attention riveted on one form of sin, that in which it appears in a class of men a thousand miles off, and denouncing that class of sinners with a vehemence and self-complacency, as if they saw in others nothing but disinterested benevolence. We should not hear so much said of depraved appetites, and so little of the causes of such depravity. It would have been generally understood before this, how appetites are depraved, by the bread which is baked for the public; by the vicious manner in which animals are fatted for the market, by vicious modes of agriculture—by fields exhausted of their strength, or forced into overbearing by rank manure, or overrun with noxious weeds. We should not have the highest authorities in agriculture, recommending the exclusive use of green manure, because it yields a greater crop, as if there were no room for the inquiry, whether the crop so yielded be not a fruitful source of disease. We should not see on some of our apparently most thriving farms, and in most healthy situations, whole families wasting away, just because the blind have been leading the blind, till both are fast falling into the ditch together.

In the blunders committed by people in regard to such matters, I seem to see plain indications, that left to themselves, they will blunder right at last. For the honor of learning, I wish to see the professions which are specially dignified with her name, do what remains to be done to set public sentiment right. Let not the malicious remark be too fully verified, that heads filled with Latin and Greek, mathematics and professional lore, are the last to admit the evidence of their own eyes, and the suggestions of plain, practical, common sense.

A FOURTH APPEAL

TO THE THREE LEARNED PROFESSIONS.

It has been objected to the supposition of the incorporated merchants in my last Appeal, that it is not exactly parallel to some cases to which it might be intended to be applied; that of the qualities of merchandize, which people buy for

their own consumption, they are far better qual-
ified to judge, than they are competent to reason
aright in regard to other interests, which have
been committed to privileged orders or faculties.
Thus the Spanish Priest would probably argue,
So complicated is the structure of the human
soul, so vast the scheme of religion, that very
few individuals in our communities know, when
they need discipline or penance ; hence "they
can never properly estimate the effects of these
remedial measures, and are constantly exposed
to be the dupes of ignorance."

I reply, first, suppose it had been beat into
people from their earliest days, that trade is
such a mysterious art, and so complex the considerations, on which the value and proper use
of articles of merchandize depend, that they
must not exercise their own judgment on the
case. Suppose it had always been inculcated,
that to deal in articles of food, requires such a
minute acquaintance with the internal structure
of the body, its functions of digestion, assimila-
tion, &c., with the Latin names of every article,
and of every part of the body to be nourished
thereby, that the art must be committed to a
corporation strictly defended from intruders.
Suppose law and public sentiment had long

stigmatized as —— fortunately we have no word to express what I was going to say ; but if the wisdom of our legislators and public sentiment had taken the course supposed, we should doubtless have had to express the occupation of the independent trader in despite of law, a word as opprobrious, as is *heresy* or *quackery*, to express independency in religion or medicine. If these suppositions had been realized, would not our people generally have been as incompetent judges of articles of merchandize, as they are to judge in regard to any of their interests ? as incompetent as the people of Spain are to judge of religious doctrines ?

I reply, secondly, supposing the people to be thus ignorant in regard to merchandize, would such ignorance probably render the imposition of the incorporated merchants more or less oppressive ? Or, supposing religion to be indeed so complicated and mysterious a subject, that people generally cannot exercise any rational judgment upon it, but must surrender reason and conscience to their priests, and detest all at variance with what they are taught by their authorized guides, as spiritual quackery ; would this be an argument, why the priests should or should not live on the vices of the people ?

Would it render it more or less dangerous to have the people pay for spiritual disease, rather than for spiritual health?

I am aware, there are qualifying considerations in regard to the conclusion to which these remarks' tend. First, there are in every profession, men, in whom the gospel has implanted a principle opposite to that selfishness, which is the general " end and aim." To overlook the exceptions would be as unphilosophical as to deny the general rule. There have always been, too, unlicensed pretenders in medicine, gaining more or less the confidence of the populace, to keep licensed practitioners from going quite to sleep. Then again the jealousy generally entertained towards the legal profession, has had its salutary influence. Many more qualifying considerations in regard to this profession might be suggested; but to do so would only be to repeat the substance of what one has already said in a Temperance Address delivered before the Bar of Oxford County, Maine. But after all, the case is very different from what it would be, if the members of the three professions generally were impelled by fervent charity to spend and be spent, for bringing about the perfection of society; or, in defect of such impulse, if interest and duty were everywhere made to coincide, and the principle of maintaining an order to live on the ignorance, vices, and distresses of the community, universally and forever abandoned.

If the clergy have not raised their voice against this practical absurdity of our social system, it must be remembered in palliation of their fault, how jealous people have been of their interesting themselves in things political or civil, or anywise aside from their more appropriate province. But I can say, from ample acquaintance, and particular inquiry, that a feeling has taken strong hold, and is fast gaining with them, that the Reformation and our own Revolution, were but different acts in the great drama of the Mind's Emancipation from profession-craft and superstition, the last and greatest of which is yet to follow. It cannot long escape acute observers, that the issue, to which I as their herald am urging matters, is but the last great battle between republican and aristocratic principles. This contest has been so often agitated on other grounds, that no doubt can remain of the result. Or rather, so weary am I of all contention, I would fain hope, that the merits of the question at issue may be so fully and forcibly urged upon the minds of those, whose unfortunate education has set them in opposition to popular rights and the perfection of the social system, that they may be induced to decline the contest as hopeless, and come over voluntarily to the side of freedom.

But if this result cannot be brought about without a degree of agitation, I believe there is yet enough of the spirit of '76 among the clergy, to furnish a host, not to shrink from responsibility. The very agitation, I believe, will serve to distinguish, who have at heart the bringing about of the best welfare of the community, and the vindication of Eternal Providence from the foul aspersions cast upon it by the present prevalence of bodies loaded with disease, and of premature death.

I have been happy to find the feeling to which I have alluded, chiefly among those, who have learned wisdom from observing, how often the cause of truth and right has been dishonored by having enlisted on its side personal animosity, party spirit, and egotism; who do not relieve people from the irksomeness of contemplating their own sins, by rousing their indignation against the sins of others; who would not have an outcry raised against slavery at a distance, to divert attention from the slavery existing nearer

home ; who, whether they contemplate the prostitution of the sacred names of *liberty* and
humanity to the gratification of senseless passion
and unhallowed ambition, or the wide spread
havoc of human life made by the combined
operation of superstition and professional pride,
seem incapable of any stronger emotion, than
" Father, forgive them, for they know not what
they do."

Such clergymen, having acted their part well
in the closing scene of the Mind's Emancipation,
may expect to find the word of God quick and
powerful in their hands to reach the hearts of
men, as they had scarcely dared hope to witness
—a change, as if the sword of the Spirit had
recovered its lost edge; or as if the Sun of
righteousness had emerged from the misty hori-
zontal air, no longer shorn of his beams.

AN APPEAL

IT appeared strange to some that the attempt made in our last legislature to abolish the monopoly enjoyed by your profession, should have been defeated, after the precedent adopted in regard to the medical profession. The fact, however, is readily explained, when we recollect your preponderance in our legislative assemblies, and the known reluctance of privileged bodies to yield their antiquated pretensions. I shall not canvass the arguments with which you resisted the late attempt to give free access to the bar. They were just those which have been used in every contest with republican principles by aristocrats and monopolists, learned ignorance and professional pride. But I wish just to call

* January, 1836.

your attention to the effect which the continuance of the present state of things will have on your own profession.

Human wisdom has ever sought to secure the respectability of its favored professions, by giving the privilege of refusing admission to those judged incompetent. The inevitable result of all such indulgence uniformly is, that the profession most securely defended by mystery and exclusive privileges, becomes a refuge for the college graduates, and other ambitious young men, who want talents and character to stand an open and honorable competition. If I wished to render a profession *not* respectable, I would take just the course which has ever been pursued so confidently for securing the opposite result.

Every practical man will admit at once the general proposition, that our best securities for rendering men faithful and efficient are, to watch them narrowly, to leave competition free, and to make interest and duty coincide. Strange that what appears so plain, should be so long in obtaining full admission in practice. I need not tell you how religion fared, when people yielded implicitly their confidence to their spiritual guides, who were constituted the sole judges whom to admit into their number, and whose revenues flowed from the vices of the people. In regard to the clergy, we have come fully into the admission of the principles above stated, and their respectability has risen and is rising accordingly.

People did not see at once, that principles evident enough in regard to religion, were equally applicable in regard to medicine. Accordingly, legislative wisdom and popular sentiment long sought to promote the respectability of the medical profession, and the efficacy of medical practice, by sustaining a monopoly, yielding implicit confidence, and stigmatizing all independence as *quackery* and *empiricism*. It was seen at last, that to legislate against quackery, is just as foolish as to legislate against heresy. Our last legislature consequently abolished the old restrictions, and so far as legislative enactments can do it, left medical practitioners to be estimated like other men, as they can satisfy people of their fidelity and skill. The result will inevitably be, that the profession will cease to be a refuge for aspiring youths, who seek to hide ignorance and inefficiency, behind professioual mystery and professional privileges. The character of the profession will rise, as much as that of the clerical profession has risen under like treatment.

Meanwhile, how is to fare the character of the legal profession? Will you insist on being alone in the privileges of a monopoly—of admitting, at your own discretion, your members? *Your* profession now (from late charges) presents the most alluring opening to ambitious ignorance and incompetence. Will you continue it thus, or will you voluntarily throw it open to that fair competition, acknowledged to be so important in all other interests?

I know that, in the debates of the last legislature, you represented the question at issue to be, whether, in practising law, a thorough preparation should be made, just as people are expected to prepare themselves competently for other business. This is not the question at all. It is, whether you, as a close corporation, shall decide, or whether the people shall be permitted to decide for themselves, who are competent to manage their causes, just as they decide in regard to their other interests.

These suggestions are made from the sincere desire of seeing your profession not lose, but gain, in respectability; and from the firm conviction, that the course suggested is the sole way to such result.

THE CIRCULAR.*

THE following is the circular to the presidents of the colleges, referred to in the second Appeal. Its publication may seem inconsistent with professions therein. But it has been thought best for the following reasons.

1. An answer from only one college has been received. It is therefore concluded, that as to the rest generally, the old rule is not to be violated, that it does not fit their dignity to notice any thing of prime importance to the welfare of the community, till public sentiment decides for it.

2. I wish to bring fully and plainly before the members of each profession, the evils among themselves requiring correction. There seems more hope of influencing those who come most

---

* See A WORD TO THE WISE, &c., Moral Reformer, Vol. I. p. 258.

into contact with general society, than those whose duties are more confined within college walls.

3. Though it would be mere affectation to suppose, that other than professional men will not read what is published for them especially, or that they will read it without sensation; yet I have judged, it might be best to lay it before the public : first, judging from all past experience, it is hardly to be expected, that any body of men will seriously set itself thoroughly to remove its own deep-rooted and long tolerated evils, till pretty closely urged by the general voice. Secondly, I have thought, that the manner, in which the cause of the people is here stated, would rather give precision and temper to their demands, than exasperate their passions.

Dorchester, Mass. June 11, 1835.

Sir,

I have some thoughts, the result of the observation and reflection of years, on the subject of general reform and social improvement, which seem to me important enough, to justify me in departing from ordinary rules, thus to address you. That temperance, and every kindred cause, are very much at a stand, I find pretty generally acknowledged. Their friends seem to be aware, that the root of the evil has not been reached, and at a loss, where to strike next. Without further preface, I beg leave to suggest to you, whether the radical difficulty be not precisely here, that about one half of our liberally educated men are educated to get their living on the ignorance, the vices, and the miseries, of the community. Our lawyers are educated, not to instruct people in the constitution and laws of the land, their rights and obligations, and to keep them out of difficulty, but to profit by the errors committed for lack of such knowledge. Our physicians are educated, not to teach people the art of preserving health, but to profit by people's ignorance of such art.

In allowing these interests to remain so much in opposition to the best welfare of the community—in confiding so much to the disinterested benevolence of men, whom, generally speaking, we cannot suppose to be animated with the spirit of Paul, to encounter evil report or good report, to spend and be spent, for the welfare of mankind—we are practically setting at defiance the divine warning, " Cursed be the man that trusteth in man ; " and practically denying the corresponding declaration, that " the heart is deceitful above all things and desperately wicked." (Jer. xvii. 5, 9.) As a community, I believe, we are suffering a tremendous penalty, for not simply taking God's word here as sober truth, and an awful reality. The present constitution of things render,it inevitable, that the professions in question should not come into measures of reform, (generally speaking,) faster than they are driven by the force of public sentiment. I complain not of them particularly. The fault belongs to the whole body of society —it exists in the general conspiracy to contradict God's charge of the all-powerful principle, by which natural men are governed. I acknowledge a qualifying consideration, so far as in every profession there are men constrained by the disinterested love of Christianity : and could the whole number be brought under the same influence, it would be the best of all remedies. But as a supplementary one, we need so to modify our social institutions, that people shall pay for knowledge, rather than be taxed for ignorance—ignorance of the organic laws, and the laws of the land. That the necessity of this will be generally seen before long, I most firmly believe : and I hold it as a thought of great importance, to be inculcated on the young men

coming forward for professional life, that times
are changing, and it behoves them not to calculate on finding people pay the tax of ignorance
so submissively as in times past but on being
the enlighteners and reformers of the age. I
wish, for the credit of learning, to see its sacred
seats directing public movements in regard to
this matter; and not resting, till public sentiment decides it; as has too often been the case
with questions of great general interest. I wish
to engage in the cause men, who will take an
enlarged, candid, and Christian view of it; and
keep clear of the anti-ism and party spirit, with
which almost every thing now is managed.
There is here no occasion for personal animosity
towards the men, whose present interests stand
in the way of the general welfare. I am but
looking ahead for difficulties, with which they
must by and by be encompassed, in this republican community, and in this restlessly inquiring
age. If the truth is not told soon by men, who
will do it kindly and candidly, it will be thun-
dered out by men, who will make it a hobby for
party organization. I wish to anticipate such
men. All my habits and feelings incline me to
shrink from coming forward as a popular leader.
For this reason precisely, I wish to see the ac-

knowledged leaders of the public mind beginning to move. But if they will refuse, I am determined, at no distant day, to appeal directly to the people—to tell them plainly, Here is the evil, and you must arise in your strength for its correction. *Flectere si nequeo superos, Acheronta movebo.*

I am not alone in the views now expressed. Several men, eminent as editors, and otherwise, have testified to me their cordial interest and acquiescence in the same. To prepare the public for what I consider as a just view of the subject, I have, since the commencement of the year, published an Address delivered before the Union Temperance Society, of Oxford County, Maine, and lately in the Boston Recorder a series of articles headed Body and Soul; which may be continued further.   Yours,

WM. WITHINGTON.

AN ADDRESS,

DELIVERED BEFORE THE UNION TEMPERANCE
SOCIETY OF OXFORD COUNTY, MAINE.

Mr. President, Ladies and Gentlemen,

THE common ground of remark on occasions like this, has been traversed so often, that I purpose to deviate a little from it, and to speak on the part taken in the Temperance Reformation by the three learned professions respectively. And intending to express my sentiments somewhat freely, I would premise distinctly, that I mean to speak of neither in the language of boasting, or compliment, or reproach. My object is to show, how the events of this reformation are developing some of the principles of human nature,—principles which we shall find always govern men taken in a body. If, therefore, in unfolding my views, I seem to speak of any class of men as deficient in that vigilance and energy which might have been expected of them in staying the plague which was desolating the land, I shall do it with the design of showing, that their conduct calls for no particular **cen-sure**; that it is resolvable into the motives, or principles, which govern mankind generally.

One who had never reflected particularly on the principles of human nature, which I intend to illustrate, if required to predict, where the crusade should originate, to be waged so justly against the destroyer,—who would lead the van in the holy warfare, would probably say, The authorized guardians of the public health, the profession which introduced alcohol as a medicine, whose prescriptions more than any thing else had given it currency, as an article of common necessity; the profession to which so implicit deference was paid by the community generally in matters within their own province; who should have best known, what evils the article was working in society, and were under so many obligations first to sound an effectual alarm, as faithful sentinels of the public health. The fact however was different. Medical books indeed told the truth plainly enough as to the evils of alcohol; and medical practitioners were not wanting to repeat the same : but the truth was generally told as some ministers tell sinners their danger and their duty, as if they expected not to be attended to. It was left to others to originate, and put into action, a bold system of measures, like men determined to do something. Not the credit, but the happiness of thus taking the lead, I believe, must be assigned to the clerical profession. Gentlemen of the bar may claim the next place in the enterprise. I know not how the case may be in this vicinity, but, I believe, no one extensively acquainted with facts will deny, that the other profession, as a body, have been manifestly behind these two in promptness and energy to discourage altogether the use of spirituous liquors. And if this be questioned, the fact that they have not been so prominently the leaders in the cause, as might have been expected of them, considered simply as the authorized guardians of the public health, will sufficiently justify the substance of what I shall say, as serving to show that what an ignorant or uncharitable observer might tax as a flagrant neglect of duty, is to be resolved simply into the universal principles of human nature.

One principle of human action thus brought to view, is, that in order to secure in men quick-sightedness and efficiency in bringing out great practical results it is all-important to make it their interest so to do, and their *present* interest too. Now the clerical profession had a present interest in devising an effectual remedy for the evils of intemperance, (apart from that love of God and man, which alone should prove an all-constraining motive,) because the immediate tendency of men's becoming temperate, is to show more respect for religion, and to support its institutions more liberally. I say a *present* interest; because, though I hope it will appear, that the worthy part of the other two professions are to find in this reformation the promotion of their interest calculated on a large scale, yet their present interest is receiving a check. For in proportion as temperance prevails, an immense source of litigation, and of disease, is cut off. Therefore the first view of things is, that the temperance reform is to prove detrimental to the legal, and to the medical profession; and the injury threatened to each seems about equal.

We must look then further for the cause, why the legal have gone before the medical profession in the cause now before us: and I seem to find it in the principle of human action, that men as a body are efficient and discerning, in proportion as they are held responsible for results to public opinion; released from which, they have a strange tendency to run wild in their speculations, to act without efficiency, or regard to plain fact and common sense; and in the fact that lawyers, much more than physicians, have always been compelled to feel, that they are responsible for the results of their practice.

Accordingly we see what a baneful influence mystery and exclusiveness have exerted on every science or subject of human thought, into which they have been carried. It has often been attempted to promote science by rich endowments and exclusive privileges, that the professors might devote themselves to the pursuit independently, without want of books or apparatus, or fear of competition, or care of providing for their daily bread. But the greatest results have been brought about, not by such means, but against the whole array of them,—in despite and in defiance of them—by men thrown on their own resources, compelled to feel that they could not sustain their credit on their books, or on their privileges;—but that all their hope was in thinking for themselves, and in bringing out some great result.*

When we review the corruptions so early in-

---

* Thus it is as true in philosophy as it is in religion, that God chooses the foolish things of the world to confound the wise, and the weak things of the world, to confound the things that are mighty.

troduced into the Christian church, so gross
and so long continued, we seem at a loss, how
Christianity could so soon become so totally
changed from what it was. At one time, we
are indignant at the villany, which could impose
such senseless doctrines and practices on the
people. At another, we wonder at the assurance, which could utter such tales, and expect
to be believed. At another, we are at a loss,
how ambition itself, cunning and aspiring as it
is, could be gratified with leading a multitude
degraded so nearly to a level with the brutes.
But in very truth the clergy of those days deserve no peculiar reproach for insincerity, har-
dihood, or stupidity. They were only acting
upon the principles, which are common to man.
The beginning of mischief was, that from the
manifestly superior learning and superior piety
of the clergy, the people respectfully yielded up
to them the sole right of deciding on religious
subjects. This easily passed into the sole right
of thinking on such subjects. The consequences were such as inevitably result from
leaving to a privileged body to reason, and
decide on a subject of general interest. Not
being responsible for results to public opinion,
they reasoned awry more and more : and thus

were introduced all the corruptions, which deformed and disgraced religion.

And as the people honored and compensated their spiritual guides, not in proportion as they were made better by their influence, but just the reverse; as the vices of the people filled the coffers of the priests with money paid for the exercise of the pardoning and dispensing power; interest was set against duty : it was not the interest of the clergy to reform abuses, and return to a simple and direct method of administering to the spiritual ills of mankind. Interest, and the short-sightedness consequent upon long irresponsibility, so perverted the judgment of the clergy, that it remained for others to discover truths so obvious, as that the kingdom of Christ is not of this world; and that the working out of one's salvation is not so mysterious a business, that the understanding and conscience must be surrendered to a professional guide.

As religion in the church, so fared philosophy in the schools, while public curiosity pried not into its secrets. Nothing can be more ingenious than the discussions there agitated about virtue and vice, entities and quiddities and the predicaments; and nothing more barren of useful results; till Bacon, (not a philosopher by profession but a statesman,) following the leading of the times, dragged philosophy from its retreats, to answer at the bar of public opinion, for the good it was effecting in the world.

Just so has fared politics, while left in the hands of a privileged body. And the constitutions of government best promoting the general welfare, have been formed, not by men born to the privilege, and trained to the art of governing; but by men selected from almost every calling, self-taught in the art of government.

Again we have an illustration of the stimulating power of responsibility, and of the paralyzing influence of exclusive privileges, in the acknowledged fact, that the clergy of an establishment are always less efficient men, than the dissenting clergy. No matter what the creed, or the form, avowed by the establishment; the result is the same. So confessedly in England. The established clergy have far the advantage as to education. (I mean *school* education; for *education* includes much more, even all I shall mention as making the dissenters what they are.) They have the countenance of the great, and the support of government. Yet the dissenting clergy are the efficient men, (generally speaking, of course.) The reason is obvious: they are under greater responsibility. They depend on their efficiency for their support. Unless too they maintain a better state of morals and religion, than exists in the establishment, the question is at once raised; What are you gaining by dissent? The clergy within the establishment may suffer religion and morals to fall some degrees below the level without, and not attract public animadversion : but not too far below, or they become subjects of general remark. Thus dissent reacts on the establishment: and what vigor exists in that, is mainly owing to the great vigor existing without.

We see the same principle brought to view, when, reviewing the history of our ancestors, we find that law, or the administration of justice, has never been so widely diverted from its proper end, as have other things of like general interest. No doubt it has been and may be still, unnecessarily complicated and mysterious. Judges under the influence of the crown have perverted justice. Juries have been intimidated, or bribed, or swayed by popular phrenzy, into an unrighteous verdict. Still, law has never been corrupted like religion. We may find a time in the history of our ancestors, when we may well doubt, whether no churches would not have been better, than the churches existing as they were. But at no period can we reasonably suppose, that the public would have been benefited by the abolition of the courts of justice.

An explanation may be found in the early institution of juries. This truly republican institution kept the business from becoming wholly a mystery in the hands of a privileged irresponsible body, or faculty. The common sense of twelve plain men had a mighty influence to keep professional learning from running wild. If the institution has proved useful as furnishing a guard to the *honesty* of judges; I believe, it has proved equally so, as a guard against judges' being bewildered in their own learning.

Another comparison between the church and the court will illustrate the power of responsibility. It will be acknowledged by careful observers, that generally speaking lawyers in their pleading, show more common sense, than ministers in their preaching. We shall hardly find a lawyer attacking any prejudice in the minds of the jury, without a plain and pressing cause for so doing; who, for instance, in addressing a jury that believed in witchcraft, would attack their belief with argument or ridicule, unless the success of his client's cause required that belief to be subverted. He would be thought strangely unskilled in his profession, who should thus arm prejudice against himself. But a clergyman thus attacking some opinion of his hearers, without thinking what he expects to persuade them to or from doing, is not a thing unheard of. Thus I have known one to belabor himself to bring his hearers to accord with him in the opinion of some speculators, that the demoniacs of the gospels were possessed of only natural maladies, spoken of as possessed of devils, in accommodation to popular opinion. What practical decision he expected them to make from the opinion, I presume, he never thought to inquire.

We shall hardly find a lawyer addressing a jury in the style of his college orations, soaring above their level, not thinking why, or under the pretence of elevating their taste. Would that a like remark might be made of the clerical profession.

Now the cause of this difference is not, that in the one profession we find better native sense, better scholarship, or more honesty, than in the other; but because the lawyer is under a more pressing responsibility. When he addresses a jury, every one knows what he has to do—to bring them to a present decision in favor of his client. If he fails of this, no matter how fine a speech he may have made—how much he may have pleased his hearers; he has failed of his main object. And if he so fails a few times, with reasonable means of success, he loses his professional reputation, and loses his support. Now, a clergyman ought never to address a congregation, without feeling his object to be, to bring them to decide a question more important, than any that can come before a jury. But he is not *compelled* so to feel. He may preach to a people month after month, or even year after year, and perhaps not an individual has done a single important act in consequence of anything he has said. But if he has met the theological views of the people, if his sermons have been handsomely written, and well delivered; if he has been agreeable in his social intercourse,— the people may think he has quitted himself well; and almost of course he takes up the same conclusion.

The principle I have been endeavoring to illustrate is, that classes of men are quick-sighted to discern what the exigencies of the times require, in proportion as their profession is not veiled in mystery, nor defended by exclusive privileges, and themselves consequently responsible to public opinion for results. Such are led to calculate their own interest on a large and liberal scale. Whereas the opposite state of things, while it may consist with a short-sighted cunning, seems to deprive men of the faculty of calculating their own interest on an extended scale. Thus it is that privileged orders, whether their privileges were political, religious, or scientific, have so generally failed to yield their antiquated pretensions to the changes of the times, as their own interest obviously requires. The case of Charles I., of Louis XVI. and his nobility, and of many other privileged exclusives, enjoying political privileges, or whatever else, may be described in the same words. A mighty current began to move beneath them. Had they yielded to it in season, they might have exerted a full share of influence on its direction, saving their credit mostly or wholly, perhaps even with increase. But they would not. They struggled against yielding an inch, till the last gasp. And then, when they would gladly have turned, and swum with the stream, it was too late : and they were plunged ten thousand fathoms beneath the surface.

The principle thus far illustrated I believe sufficiently shows, why the profession which I have the honor to address, has seized on the decision, required by the exigency of the times, in regard to ardent spirit, with more promptness generally, than has been manifested by the faculty of medicine. I find the cause in the fact, that your profession is eminently calculated to render you *practical* men. It is not wrapped up in mystery. It is your daily business to clear up its intricacies and mysteries to the apprehension of common men. And your employers can calculate very exactly how well you execute your trust.

The medical faculty have wanted this exercise for keeping open eyes, to mark the signs of the times, and seize the present exigency. The profession has long been considered as so mysterious, and submitted so exclusively to the judgment of its professors, as to require implicit deference on the part of the employer. Whether there are radical defects in the prevailing practice, whether in any instance a patient has died through wrong treatment, or recovered with a constitution so impaired by medicine, that it would have been safer on the whole to have trusted wholly to nature and nursing, to work a cure, have been considered as questions, which it would be presumptuous for the uninitiated to ask. And we have very absurdly withheld from medical practitioners the strong stimulus of self-interest to devise a simple, safe, and thorough method of curing disease. For instead of securing our bodies against disease, as we secure our houses against fire; paying the physician a premium to warrant our health and requiring him to forfeit a prescribed sum for every day's sickness, 'we have done just the reverse: we have paid for sickness, and not for health. And it would be very strange, if interest set against duty did not here exert the paralyzing influence so manifest in all other cases.

The wisdom of our legislators also has thought to secure the efficiency of medical practice by laws giving exclusive privileges to the regularly licensed practitioner; as in some countries the like has been attempted in regard to religion, by establishing a church with its law-supported, law-protected clergy; the same reason being assigned in both cases, the necessity of protecting people against ignorant pretenders. Well there is a period of society when it may be best to have an established church defended by some exclusive privileges. But the time comes, when this must be thrown aside, all denominations put on a level, and every one left free and unrestrained to think on the subject of religion. And although at such a time we may expect many to abuse their liberty to licentiousness, many wild errors to be broached, and have their vogue, and many to be imposed upon by false pretenders; yet we may expect, that such errors will soon reach their maturity and die away, and that all things are hastening to the ultimate purity of truth, and to the full development of the energies of undefiled religion.

I think, that a parallel may here be found between the science relating to the health of our souls, and that which relates to the health of our bodies. If I mistake not, it is the misfortune of physicians of our day, to live at a period, when public sentiment is loudly demanding a great change in the means of preserving health; and that like all classes of men, accustomed to exclusive privileges, and implicit deference, they have been a little slow in discerning what the exigency of the times requires. Thus I explain, why they have been somewhat behind the legal profession in the temperance cause.

As an instance of this falling behind the general sense of the community, I might mention the fact, that after public sentiment became pretty decided against the use of ardent spirit, it began to be seriously inquired by some of the medical faculty, whether it might not be wholly dispensed with in medicine; and for a substitute, opium seems to have been chiefly depended on. Opium however is more decidedly a poison than alcohol. But. is it liable to the same abuse as an intoxicating drug? Let Turkey, or almost any nation of Southern Asia answer. Let China answer, how rapidly within a few years, in despite of the severest interdicts of the emperor, it has there come into general use, slaying and debilitating beyond even the pretensions of alcohol here in the days of its glory.

I think, we here have an instance, how apt professional reasoning, not accustomed to submit itself to the plain common sense of mankind, is to run counter to that sense. This says, resist the beginnings of evil. When spirit was introduced as the occasional cordial, or the exhilarating pledge, O that the men of that day could have been aware of its true character and tendency, and crushed the serpent still young. A little effort then might have availed more than a great deal of labor now. All mischief resembles strife in its likeness to the letting out of water. At first, one man with his shovel, can easily stop the breach; it is soon a flood, and to repair its ravages, costs the labor of years.

But professional reasoners have not been wanting, who should seem to argue thus : Now that the evils of ardent spirit, have been fairly laid before the public, and it is not found in reputable society as a beverage ; since they who drink it betray, by their manner of so doing, their consciousness of degradation ; and since its entering into a medical prescription raises the query, is it necessary ? since, in short, the whole truth as to the use of spirit is so well understood, that evil example can hardly be called dangerous ; now it is time seriously to agitate the inquiry, whether it may not be banished from medicine. But as people are not generally aware of the nature of opium, of its dreadful ravages wherever men have acquired that taste for it, best acquired by often taking it as a medicine ; therefore no danger is to be apprehended, from silently introducing it to supply the place of spirit in medicine, lest it come to supply its place as the desolating scourge of our land.

Such reasoning would hardly escape from men accustomed to have their arguments canvassed before a jury. It may very well be com-

pared with theirs, who in an age, when the evils
of clerical dominion have been fully discussed
and pointed out, and in a country, all whose
institutions are levelled against such dominion,
are sounding an alarm against the strides of the
clergy towards power, and against a union of
Church and State. Or to make the parallel
perfect, the acuteness of these alarmists should
be united with the simplicity of the early be-
lievers, who, in yielding all power to the clergy,
saw only its safety from abuse in so holy hands.

I hope, I have rendered myself sufficiently intelligible ; and that you see, how the fact as to
the standing of the two secular professions with
regard to the temperance cause affords no
ground for compliment on the one hand, or for
reproach on the other; that it is but the development of one of the universal principles of
human nature,—the principle, that however exclusive privileges may foster any science or
subject of human thought in its infancy ; before
it reaches its perfection these must be done
away ; it must be stripped of mystery, left to free
thought, free discussion, free action ; or in other
words, it must be based on true republican principles ; that real republicanism is not more the

perfection of civil government, than of religion, and every other subject of general interest.

I have entered upon this discussion, because I think it affords some suggestions, especially to men young in the practice of law or medicine, or to those about entering on professional studies, which suggestions I offer from the sincerest conviction of their importance to your welfare. You see, how fast the progress of temperance is diminishing the business of managing the litigations, and of administering to the diseases of men ; while at the same time ample fields for the exertion of talent are opening in other directions. We have too long talked of the three learned professions, as if there were no other worthy men of collegiate education. But as men, by becoming more temperate, save in the expenses of litigation and of sickness, they will become more able, and more willing, to encourage talent in other directions. The expense saved by totally disusing ardent spirit, would make annually many miles of railroad and canal. Here is one of the most fit objects, to which to appropriate the money so saved. Thus a way is opening for the employment of a body of civil engineers. Is not the occupation worthy the attention of more of our liberally educated men ?

And then again, people are waking up to the importance of the general extension of a more thorough system of education. The business of teaching youth has been too long made a stepping stone to something else; and it seems to me as if Providence were diminishing the call for men in two of the professions, on purpose, that more of our college graduates might devote themselves for life to the business of teaching.

None need fear wanting employment, who will only throw themselves on the current of the times, and be up to what the spirit of the age demands. A few years have produced a great change in the clergyman's situation. He no longer stands on undisputed ground, able to get along pretty well, by composing and delivering his two sermons a week, and not notoriously violating the proprieties of his calling. He is obliged to keep a good look out, lest others go before him in a practical understanding of what the exigencies of the church require. He must find his happiness, if at all, in forgetting his private concerns, and identifying his desires with the best happiness of his people.

A call to do the like, seems now to be made by the providence of God on each profession. If so, he who makes it, will not disappoint those

who accept it in sincerity and in truth. Perhaps
the time is not distant, when much of the learning, which has been acquired for the purpose of
pleading causes, and of administering to disease,
will be demanded for lyceums in lectures. And
a town which should so reform its morals as to
afford an inadequate support for its lawyer and
its physician, we may presume would have intellectual appetite enough, and means abundant,
to maintain a lyceum, and employ and compensate a lecturer on constitutional law and kindred
subjects, and another on natural history and the
means of preserving health.*

There are signs of the times, which indicate,
that such suggestions are more especially deserving the attention of young men engaged in the
study of medicine or contemplating so to do.
Medical writers have abundantly confessed their
doubts, whether, after all the discoveries made
in their art for centuries, diseases are better
cured, than when the art was in its infancy;
and this question people are beginning to decide
for themselves. The opinion is fast gaining
ground, that if we mean to enjoy health, our
main dependence under God must be in carry-

* I might add, to be employed also at a fixed salary to administer to the sickness, more or less, in a given district.

ing out the principles of the temperance reformation, in banishing from our tables their accumulated luxuries, and returning to a simple and
moderate diet; and in a proper attention to exercise, clothing, and guarding against indiscreet
exposure; in becoming temperate in all things.
The opinion is gaining ground, that as in other
things the wants of nature are easily and obviously met, and truth on subjects of general
interest found at last to be simple and intelligible to common capacities, so if we will return to
a natural mode of living, our diseases will be
such as common experience can prescribe for,
from a knowledge of the simples of our own
woods and fields; and that we shall be under no
necessity of ransacking the bowels of every land
for drugs of dangerous character and doubtful
operation.

I can anticipate nothing else from the increasing notoriety of the fact familiar to all who have
looked into medical history, that new diseases
have been originated, and old diseases aggravated, pretty nearly in proportion as medical
science has become refined, and as new and
deadlier poisons have been introduced into the
practice, till the matter found its *ne plus ultra*
in the cholera. There are many striking facts

of this kind in medical history, upon which people are beginning to put their own construction. For instance, there is a disease peculiarly the object of horror, and for which mercury is eminently considered as a specific. But no mention of that disease is found in history, till just about the time when mercury was introduced into medicine. I need not enlarge on such a fact, or suggest the importance of the inquiry, how far the disease has been created by mercury. A word to the wise is sufficient.

There is another fact too much in point, and too deeply concerning all interested in the domestic relation, to allow me to refrain from alluding to it through a false delicacy. So far as I have inquired, the fact is confirmed by the testimony of all, who are old enough to be competent witnesses. In our country fifty or sixty years ago, a branch of medical practice peculiarly interesting to the fairer half of our race was wholly in the hands of their own sex. It was then comparatively easy and safe; while it has become difficult and dangerous in proportion as it has fallen into the hands of professional men, and as they have refined in their art. The experience of the whole world coincides with this tale; and I speak after careful examination, when I say, that a suspicion is fast spreading through the community, that the present melancholy frequency of death and debilitated constitutions among our ladies from the sufferings peculiar to their sex, has been the legitimate result of committing so great an outrage on common sense and common decency, as to suppose, that the most universal of nature's operations cannot be performed without other assistance than the delicate hands, to which it so appropriately belongs.*

The opinion is thus gaining currency, that there is a radical fault in the present method of giving poisonous drugs for restoring health, implanting one disease to expel another, and making devil cast out devil. It is beginning to be suspected, that this is to the body, what the principle always assumed by the heathen moralists was to the soul, namely, that one evil passion must be encouraged and strengthened, to counteract another. And as Christianity, in opposition to this, inculcates a few simple principles

---

* God has promised, that women " shall be saved in child-bearing, if they continue in faith, and charity, and holiness, with sobriety." (1 Tim. i. 15.) Surely a want of these graces is too plainly indicated by the present state of society.

as the sole and sufficient remedy for sin and vice of every kind ; a like simplicity, it is suspected, will be developed in medicine ; that the art of treating the diseases of the body will be found as simple and easy, as to administer to the diseases of the soul ; Wash and be clean ; Believe and be saved ; as simple and easy, as administering to the ills of the body politic ; Leave to an enlightened people the whole control of affairs, and away with standing army and established church, crown and coronet together. If the case be not found to be so, I do not readily see, how we shall free the Author of nature from the charge of forgetting for once the usual analogies of his wisdom and goodness.

It is not long since I heard the opinion avowed by a gentleman, who had regularly studied the profession of medicine, and practiced the art, that the strong medicines, so called, however they may remove disease, do it at so great an expense to the constitution, that it would be a saving of life, on the whole, to dispense with them entirely, and use no means but common nursing. The gentleman is well known to the public as a writer and popular editor : and if I mistake not, his opinion is so fast gaining currency, that at no distant period many drugs in our apothecaries' shops will go down, to seek the shades of brotl.er Alcohol, in the tomb of the Capulets.

I am sensible that I have called up questions which some may think, might better be suffered to rest. I reply, there is no possibility of leaving them at rest; the spirit of the times is calling them up. I have thought it an act of kindness to warn those who are expecting to spend their lives in the practice of medicine, that the spirit of popular inquiry which has been overhauling everything else, and stripping away mystery and exclusive pretensions, will not long leave their profession at rest, on its old foundations; it will subject it to the scrutiny, which has been applied to every other subject of general interest, and with such salutary effect; for it begins to be considered as a law of the human mind, that no science will be brought to anything like perfection, while made a mystery in the hands of a privileged order.*

---

* In the Boston Medical and Surgical Journal, for Sept. 17, 1834, is the following passage; " Are tea and coffee injurious ?—A person who has been some twenty, thirty, or forty years in the habit of taking these beverages, would probably lose more than gain by abandoning them.—It would be a question however, whether the former (the milk and water drinker) would be a happier

I invite you then, young physician, medical student, or whoever is contemplating to study the science, to consider whether the indications of the times do not require something else, than going the old round of dealing out calomel and opium to broken down constitutions; whether your only hope does not lie in aiming whither the tendencies of the age tend, to bring people

---

or more useful man; whether, in fact, he would not be a milk and water character." In the same work for Oct. 5th, 1824, the following information is given for literary men; " In hot weather when the system is subjected to the relaxing influence of continued heat, a little brandy and water *with* dinner will be salutary." Again (Sept. 7th, 1824.) " By the continued heat of summer we are predisposed to diseases of the bowels, and these diseases can only be prevented, and that disposition overcome by a warm and bracing diet, and the occasional use of good old wine, or weak brandy and water." When public sentiment shall have become sufficiently decided for that conclusion in regard to the common narcotic and stimulating drinks, to which practical men are everywhere coming, perhaps some seventy-five physicians of Boston may venture upon the united declaration, that *Tea and Coffee, as drinks, are never useful for men in health.* Thus among the *Principles of the Temperance Reformation,* I include as a most important one, the assertion of a right on the part of the people to go before their authorized guardians in matters of reform. Let them accordingly beware, lest Alcohol be made a scape-goat to bear away the sins of all his fellows.

generally so to understand the art of preserving health, that it shall be seldom impaired beyond their own knowledge to administer the means of cure.

Having had some occasion to look into medical history, to mark the contradictory theories, which have risen and fallen, one before another, in such rapid succession, the darkness which broods over the subject by the confession of all; I cannot but greet the growing disposition to regard the extension of the principles of the temperance reformation into all things as the great means of forestalling and resisting dyspepsy and other diseases. I greet it in the language of Milton, 'Hail, holy light, offspring of heaven first born.' I greet it, as a meet accompaniment of the operations which are tending to restore the jarring elements of the world, to the rule of the Prince of peace; as an indication of the approach of the time, of which it is promised, that " As the days of a tree shall be the days of my people;" no longer like the grass of the field, no longer like the fading flower; when the inhabitants of the land shall no more say, I am sick, and when the infant shall die an hundred years old. And as one remarkable phenomenon of the religious world now is, that the frequent occurrence of premature death seems to have lost its tendency to affect the survivors with a salutary sense of their own mortality, but too frequently to tend to just the reverse; so as friends of Christianity we seem invited to welcome any means, which promise to free us from the necessity of pronouncing so often prematurely that farewell

> Which ends all earthly friendships,
> And closes every feast of love.

If my suggestions are worth nothing, let them pass by. I speak as to wise men. Judge ye what I say.

APPENDIX.

Since this address has been in the hands of the publisher, I have read, for the first time, Spurzheim on Education. A few extracts will show, how well some of his sentiments accord with mine.

"Among the abuses concerning rewards and distinctions, I mention only the fault to give to regular professors the exclusive right of teaching. Monopoly impedes improvement in everything." p. 180.

"A great step towards perfection, would be the full and practical admission of the principle, that every one has the right to employ his talents to the utmost, for his own benefit, as far as he can do it without injuring others. This system of government is certainly superior to that of exclusive privileges of any kind." p. 182.

"This study (*Materia Medica*) will not require great extension, if we attend more to the art of healing than to the display of knowledge. The most skillful practitioners use a small number of drugs in curing their patients, and they use still less for themselves, being indisposed." p. 202.

"The members of the ordinary professions do not think it necessary to conceal, that the end and aim of all their exertions is selfishness. The same anti-social principle is visible in all worldly affairs.—This overwhelming flood of selfishness must abate, or the general happiness of mankind remain an impossibility." p. 271.

If further authority of like import is wanted, the following may serve as a specimen out of an abundance.

"By what unaccountable perversity in our frame does it appear, that we set ourselves so much against any thing that is new? Can any one behold, without scorn, such droves of physicians, and after the space of so many hundred years experience and practice of their predecessors, not one single medicine has been detected, that has the least force directly to prevent, to oppose, and expel a continued fever? Should any, by a more sedulous observation, pretend to make the least step towards the discovery of such remedies, their hatred and envy would swell against him, as a legion of devils against virtue, the whole society will dart their malice at him, and torture him with all the calumnies imaginable, without sticking at anything that should destroy him root and branch.

For he who professes to be a reformer of the art of physic, must resolve to run the hazard of the martyrdom of his reputation, life and estate."—*Dr. Harvey.*

" As matters stand at present, it is easier to cheat a man out of his life than of a shilling, and almost impossible either to detect or punish the offender. Notwithstanding this, people still shut their eyes, and take everything upon trust that is administered by any pretender to medicine, without daring to ask a reason for any part of his conduct. Implicit faith, every where else the subject of ridicule, is still sacred here. Many of the faculty are no doubt worthy of all the confidence that can be reposed in them ; but as this can never be the character of every individual in any profession, it would certainly be for the safety, as well as the honor of mankind, to have some check on the conduct of those, to whom they intrust so valuable a treasure as health."

* * * * * * * *

" Very few of the valuable discoveries in medicine have been made by physicians. They have in general either been the effect of chance or of necessity, and have been usually opposed by the faculty, till every one else was convinced of their importance. An implicit faith in the opinions of teachers, an attachment to systems and established forms, and the dread of reflections, will always operate upon those who follow medicine as a trade. Few improvements are to be expected from a man, who might ruin his character and family, by even the smallest deviation from an established rule."

* * * * * * * *

" ' No argument,' continues he,* ' can be brought

* The author of Observations on the Duties and Offices of a Physician, just quoted.

against laying open medicine, which does not apply with equal, if not greater force, to religion; yet experience has shown that since the laity have asserted their right of inquiry into these subjects, theology, considered as a science, has been improved, the interests of real religion have been promoted, and the clergy have become a more learned, a more useful, and a more respectable body of men, than they ever were in the days of their greatest power and splendor.'

"Had other medical writers been as honest as this gentleman, the art had been on a very different footing at this day. Most of them extol the merit of those men, who brought Philosophy out of the schools, and subjected it to the rules of common sense. But they never consider, that Medicine, at present, is in nearly the same situation, that philosophy was at that time, and that it might be as much improved by being treated in the same manner."—*Dr. Buchan.*

"There has been much difference of opinion among philosophers in regard to the place, which medicine is entitled to hold among the physical sciences; for while one has maintained, that it 'rests upon an eternal basis, and has within it the power of rising to perfection,' it has been distinctly asserted by another, that 'almost the only resource of medicine, is the art of conjecturing.' 'The following apologue,' says D'Alembert, 'made by a physician, a man of wit and of philosophy, represents well the state of the science. "Nature," says he, "is fighting with disease; a blind man armed with a club, i. e. the physician, comes to settle the difference. He first tries to make peace; when he cannot accomplish this, he lifts his club, and strikes at random; if he strikes the disease, he kills the

disease; if he strikes nature, he kills nature." '
' An eminent physician,' says the same writer, ' re-
nouncing a practice which he had exercised for 30
years, said, I am weary with guessing.'"—*Dr.
Abercrombie.*

" Medical science is like a temple unroofed at
the top, and cracked at the foundation."—*Dr. Rush.*

" If we take a retrospective view of the science
of medicine, with its alterations and improvements
in the last two centuries, the medical annals of this
period will present us with a series of learned dis-
sertations by authors, whose names alone are now
remembered; while their writings, under the spe-
cious name of *improvement,* have left us only the
deplorable consolation of knowing, that their works
have heaped system upon system, prescript upon
prescript, error upon error, each in turn yielding to
its follower. Year after year produces a new
advocate for a new theory of disease, each con-
demning its predecessor, and each alike to be condemned by its successor. We wish a more rational
mode adopted for the promotion of medical knowledge, than hair-brained theories and doubtful facts.
Observation must take the place of scholastic
learning and hard names. We must have facts
instead of opinions, reason instead of theory, knowledge instead of titles and certificates."—*New York
Medical Inquirer, Vol. I. No.* 1.

" Wealth may purchase the honor [of a medical
diploma], the influence of friends may secure it, or
dogged resolution, in attending three or four courses
of lectures, will at length weary out the patience of
professors, and enable the veriest dunce in the
universe to carry off the prize—it [the diploma]

amounts simply to show, that the persons who wear this distinguished honor, have been able to raise the means to attend two courses of lectures.

"This is a fair representation of that system of instruction, that is pursued in every medical college in the United States. * * * * We appeal to the public to say, if it is not one of the greatest impositions ever palmed upon an enlightened age ; if it is not perfectly *inadequate* to the object in view, and at least five centuries behind the present condition of literary improvement."—*Western Journal of the Medical and Physical Sciences.*

"The abuses of these [the heroic] remedies, and the abundant use of even mild articles in endless combinations, too often witnessed among us, cannot be too openly, nor too loudly reprobated. These errors are disgraceful to our profession. But if that were all, one might be silent. They cause endless, and often great suffering to those, who are already afflicted enough."—*Dr. Jackson.*

"To a certain extent I have seen demonstrated the actual benefit of certain modes of treatment in acute diseases. But is the benefit immense? When life is threatened do we often save it? When a disease is destined by nature to be long, do we often very materially diminish it? I doubt not that we sometimes do under certain circumstances. But on the other hand, I must acknowledge, that what I have seen here,* of disease and its issues, has rather inclined me to believe, that *I individually* overvalued the utility of certain modes of treatment in America.

"I believe, that we admit many things in America as axioms, which are very far from being

---

* In Paris.

proved. We have too long believed, that, because demonstration on many points was impossible in medicine, it was not worth while to study it like an exact science.

"For shame upon us, that the antiquarian can spend years of toil and labor to decypher an Egyptian hieroglyphic, the naturalist a life of hardship and privations to ascertain minute points of no practical interest, and that we should pass our lives *getting money*, when, by study and devotion to what is intrinsically of equal interest, simply as an exercise of the human mind, we could reach such results of essential importance, to the happiness of millions.

"The reason that medicine * * * is so despised as a science is, that it has never yet been studied as a *science*.

"Is it enough for me to know what the books can teach me? They contain more falsehood than truth; and I cannot distinguish between them without studying nature."—*James Jackson, Jr., M. D.*

Such is medical science and medical practice, according to the authority of those most interested to make a favorable report; such the jugglery played off upon fashion and legislative wisdom, popular ignorance and science falsely so called. Truly poor human wisdom seems destined to go the same round of folly in regard to every general interest, before hitting upon the right course, namely, the full and practical admission, that "equal rights should be secured to all, and exclusive privileges to none"*—that our best securities for rendering men faithful and efficient are, to watch

* Governor Davis's Speech to the Legislature of Massachusetts, January 13, 1835.

them narrowly, to leave competition free, and to make interest and duty coincide.

It is common indeed, to represent the confessed darkness of medical science as necessarily attached to the inherent difficulties of the subject; one instance among a million, in which men charge upon God the consequences of their own fault, for the alternative is simply, whether God in constituting the human body, with the means of its health, has compelled the sons of Æsculapius to float forever on the dark sea of uncertainties, or whether human folly and wickedness have attempted to make a complicated and mysterious art out of what God had made plain and simple.

TRUE CHRISTIANITY TRUE RADI-CALISM.

" In theorizing on the subject before us, even wise and good men have often mistaken first principles ; and hence the disappointment of their fondest hopes, hence the failure of their best endeavors to mitigate the evils of" society. " They have not taken man as he is, a fallen, depraved creature, naturally proud, indolent, evil and unthankful; but as he should be, holy, humble, industrious, conscientiously disposed to do every thing in his power to " mitigate the sufferings of his fellows.—*President Humphrey.*

*Cuique in sua arte credendum,** is the maxim of ordinary minds.   It is an epitome of the conservative creed.   *Cuique in sua arte credendum* how should an obscure German monk pretend to understand the Scriptures better than all the learned doctors and endowed universities of the church?   *Cuique in sua arte credendum ·* whether God has made the sun to revolve round the earth, or the earth round the sun, who should best know, the upstart Galileo, or God's own vicegerent on earth—the infallible interpreter of

---

* Every one to be trusted in his own trade.

his will? *Cuique in sua arte credendum:* how should a poor self-taught Genoese pilot presume to make discoveries to put to shame all the learned heads, which have gone before him? *Cuique in sua arte credendum:* how should the lawyers, merchants, and yeomen of America, pretend to reverse the decisions of the heads of the mother country, born to the right, and trained to the art of governing? *Cuique in sua arte credendum:* if the old institutions of Europe require reforming, leave the work to those practised in the business of government; and let not others be agitated by the discussion of matters which they do not understand.

Such are the true principles of the conservative creed. Thank God, a spirit like Luther, Columbus, or Jefferson, occasionally arises, to set its fundamental maxim at defiance: and in defiance of it every radical improvement and capital discovery has been brought about. Did I not know, from the record of all past history, how deeply rooted are conservative principles in human nature, how slow mankind are to learn the simplest practical truths, and to open their eyes upon the most glaring practical absurdities, with which they have always been familiar; I should now stand in astonishment at the spectacle of a people exulting in their freedom from the impositions of past ages, and tremblingly sensitive to vindicate their right, in all things to think and act for themselves; yet sustaining two powerful interests to thrive on their own degradation; and in regard to one of them especially, acting as if it were a shame to exercise their own judgment.

I would not excite ill will towards any class of men, as if they were governed by worse principles than are common to man. But while I regard the Bible as containing the truest philosophy of human nature, and while I behold this philosophy verified by all history, all observation, and all experience; I expect to see every experiment verify the general proposition, that, men acting in a body, no degree of learning and ingenuity, sense of honor and feeling of humanity, is sufficient to set them right, while it is their interest to go wrong, and while they can hide ignorance, inefficiency and dishonesty behind professional mystery, professional rules, and professional privileges. The proposition is so mortifying to human pride, that I do not wonder it has been so often practically denied; and hence the results so grievously different from the anticipations, when human wisdom has thought to secure the obvious advantages of the division of labor.

In accordance with the forestated principle, if I knew, that in any state religion was treated as a subject too difficult for people to exercise a free judgment upon, but was committed exclusively to the care of priests, and the priests to receive their compensation in the penalties paid by the people for vices, and that independency in religion was stigmatized as *heresy* or *schism ;* I should expect the *priests* to present the most formidable obstacle to the improvement of the people in morals beyond a certain point. I should expect them to labor heartily to keep the people from sinking to the lowest depths of depravity, lest their moral sense should become so extinct, that they should not care to atone for their sins, by purchasing peace of their spiritual guides. I should expect them, in short, to keep alive just so much sensibility of conscience, as would best render themselves objects of blind veneration and most bountifully fill their coffers. And though the priesthood might originate in men of a self-sacrificing spirit, whom the confidence reposed in them would only render more tremblingly conscientious not to abuse that confidence; I should still expect no different ultimate result, from the temptation held out to men of an opposite spirit, to insinuate themselves into the office. All this I should so unhesitatingly anticipate from leaving implicitly trusted spiritual physicians to find their account in the multiplication of spiritual disease, that I should hardly think it necessary to examine, whether the result verified the anticipation.

If I knew that in any country, legislation very much, and jurisprudence altogether, fell into the hands of men, who lived on the quarrels of the people, and the difficulties into which they fell from the perplexities and uncertainties of law; I should not expect such men to go far ahead of public sentiment for reforming manners, and bringing about the perfection of the social system : I should expect to find the " uncertainty of the law " tenfold more " glorious " than necessity requires.

If I knew that in any country the people paid their physicians for sickness, and not for health; and that the physicians were a regularly organized body, governed by their own rules; that all independency in medicine was stigmatized as *quackery;* and that the best prepared for death or life were afraid to die and ashamed to survive from a disease not treated by those supposed to have a divine and exclusive right so to do. I should expect —— I should expect, in short, that where people were papists in regard to the body, the results would exactly correspond with those, which spiritual popery has everywhere so legitimately produced.

So I should reason *a priori*. I might add, that when I reason in the contrary direction, all my observation brings me to the same conclusion. So stubborn and multiplied do the plain facts appear, that I should be obliged to admit the conclusion, however confounded by it, and unable to reconcile it with known laws of the human mind.

But it has been objected to a part of the conclusion, that though disease confessedly rages worse, and proves more unmanageable, than when medical science was in its infancy; yet the science has really been advanced towards improvement, only vicious habits of living have more than counteracted the advantages of improved skill. The objection, however just, affects not my main end. The case is as if a New England clergyman should visit Cuba for the improvement of his health, and witnessing the low state of morals, should remonstrate with one of the priests to this effect. Don't you see, that the accumulated rites, which you have been adding to religion, have been worse than useless? People are evidently less conscientious and virtuous, than when the ordinances of religion were administered to them in their primitive simplicity. The priest admits the fact, but still insists, that the multiplied rites and accumulated mystery have had a salutary tendency, only they have been more than counteracted by bull-fights, concubinage, and other devices of Satan for corrupting the people. The New Englander inquires, whether the priests have remonstrated against these satanic devices; and finds, that they have indeed done so, but for the most part formally and officially, and as if they expected not to be regarded. Further investigation shows him, that the priests are about as often at bull-fights, and keep about as many concubines, as the people themselves.

In neither case does the objection affect my main end: because I am not determining, whether, where conscience is seared and intellect blinded, as in most papal countries, the accumulated rites and mysteries of religion increase or diminish the evil, or which way the evil is affected by the popular medicines, where it is fashionable for people to live in gross ignorance

of the laws of their being. My main end is to
expose the mischief (wherever precisely it may
lie) of sustaining monopolies, and having people
taxed for ignorance, rather than pay for know
ledge.

But it is objected, such delusion, as here seems
supposed, cannot be in this enlightened age—
this age of unlimited inquiry and independent
thought—this age of overhauling the decisions
of other days. Not quite so fast. In this very
vaunting of liberality, freedom, and independence,
I see a sign that the clear day of emancipation
from superstition and prejudice, has but half
risen upon us : for true independence of mind,
like true charity, "vaunteth not itself." I have
seen in our day, something very like the account
which Paul gives of some would-be liberals at
Corinth. Let us attend a moment to the history
of their case.

Among the people converted from heathenism
to Christianity at Corinth, different views pre-
vailed as to the gods, which they had formerly
worshipped. Some regarded them as evil spirits;
their idols as the images and representatives of
such evil spirits : and consequently all respect
shown to such idols, by eating meat offered to
them, or in any other way, as an acknowledg-

ment of the divinity and dominion of such evil spirits, and consequently an act of rebellion against Jehovah.

Others took a different view of their former gods: they said, that an " idol is nothing in the world : " that the so-called gentile gods were not evil spirits, but no existences—mere creatures of the imagination. As was very natural, they prided themselves on taking a more philosophical view of the matter, than that entertained by their weaker brethren, who retained a " conscience of the idol," or regarded the idols as representing real beings—demons—evil spirits. An inference from this philosophy was, that they might safely eat meat offered in sacrifice to an idol, even in the idol's temple ; because in their hearts they paid no respect to false gods, believing, that the so-called false gods were no existences—that an idol was nothing in the world.

They overlooked the obvious consideration, that however safe such conduct might be for themselves considered alone, it was wrongly laying a dangerous snare for their weaker brethren, as they regarded them, thus tempted to violate conscience by eating also, what they could only regard as meat offered to real demons. When men began thus to impose on themselves by false reasoning—to enter upon forbidden ground, it was not singular, if they erred from Christian simplicity to an extent, which might seem hardly credible. At the worship of the heathen temples, scenes were acted, in reference to which Paul well says, that it is a shame even to speak of the things, which are done of them in secret: and of all places, Corinth was noted for such licentious abominations. Is it possible, that in the searching times of apostolic preaching, any could have yielded to a temptation so gross? Yes: when men once swerve from Christian simplicity, by listening to the refinements of a false philosophy, the downward course is rapid to the very filth and dregs of corruption. They come to justify gross guilt by investing it in smooth language. Thus it was with some called Christians at Corinth. " Meats for the belly, and the belly for meats:" said they. (1 Cor. vi. 13.) I need not say, which of the appetites, and what mode of gratification, they meant to plead for by such language. The apostle's answer, which immediately follows, sufficiently explains the meaning.

The obscenities practised in almost all heathen religions, have had their origin too, in philosophic speculations. They have been introduced as apt representations of the fructifying powers of nature. Thus it is supposed, that the fable of the wounding * of Adonis, (called *Tammuz* in Scripture,) and the consequent grief of Venus, (commemorated by the women weeping for Tammuz,) was originally intended to represent the sun deprived of his generating power by his southern declension, and the consequent sad appearance of nature during the winter months. And a modern philosopher,† speaks very contemptuously of the abhorrence expressed by the Christian missionaries for the obscenities exhibited in the heathen rites, because these were first introduced as mystic representations of the fructifying power of the sun, and the corresponding capacities of the earth : just as if the original pretence were more important, than the actual effect of such exhibitions on the imaginations of man's heart, which are evil from his youth.

Such were the circumstances of those, whom Paul reminded, that no temptation had taken them, but such as is common to man. (1 Cor. x. 13.) He compared their case with that of the ancient Israelites in the wilderness, where so many fell under the temptations besetting them.

---

* In partibus virilibus.   † Dupuis.

"Now these things," says he, "were our examples, to the intent that we should not lust after evil things, as they also lusted. Neither be ye idolaters, as were some of them; as it is written, The people sat down to eat and drink, and rose up to play. Neither let us commit fornication, as some of them also committed, and fell in one day three and twenty thousand. Neither let us tempt Christ, as some of them also tempted, and were destroyed of serpents. Neither murmur ye, as some of them also murmured, and were destroyed of the destroyer." (v. 5—10.)

Some of the things here enumerated are obviously temptations, which always and everywhere are common to man. But the idolatry here alluded to, the worship of the golden calf, might seem an exception. What temptation have we, and millions of others, to such an act? The commonness however is to be found, not in the particular act, but in the principle, on which it was recommended The Egyptians, among whom the Israelites had so long resided, were then regarded as the most refined and philosophic people on the earth. It was a part of their philosophy, that the invisible God is best worshipped by the aid to the imagination of some visible representation : and none was more common than the ox or bull, which for his strength and useful qualities was supposed to represent some of the most important attributes of the invisible Deity. Thus the temptation to the Israelites to represent the God, who had brought them out of Egypt, under the similitude of a calf or bullock, was essentially a temptation to set aside the positive word of God, the evidence of plain fact, and the dictate of common sense, from deference to the speculations of those, whom the world admired as most wise, refined, or philosophic.*

What Paul then designates as the temptation *anthropinos*, that which is common to man, is just this, the temptation to swerve from a strict regard to what God, or conscience, the evidence of sense, or unprejudiced reason, dictates, from regard to what is fashionable among those reputed great or wise in the world. The fashions and maxims of the world so change, that we cease to be tempted to the particular wrong acts, into which there was once the greatest danger of

---

* This plain statement of the case entirely refutes the papists' defence of their images, that they regard them not as divinities, but as representations of unseen objects of adoration. This was precisely the idolatry contemplated by God, in the second commandment.

falling. But the pride of fashion still arrays itself against the simple truth of God, and the dictates of unbiased conscience, and unsophisticated judgment : and to fear to be singular or unfashionable, rather than fear to go wrong—a foolish fear of being spoken of as having a better heart than head, as a well-meaning but weak-minded person—here is the temptation, eminently that which is common to man.

It might be expressed in other words, by saying, it is the temptation to assume a *false*, at the sacrifice of a *true* independence. Or in other words still, we everywhere see men tempted too successfully to strive vainly to cast off their dependence on God and the appearance of implicitly and seriously regarding his word, at the cost of making themselves slavishly dependent on the changeable breath of their fellow worms.

What multitudes there are vaunting their freedom from authority in religion, who have never thought on the subject, so as to form an opinion for themselves, fearlessly, but with the fear of rejecting the truth; independently, but with the feeling that God only is worthy to be depended on : not afraid to embrace one truth, because it is so old, as to be derided as going out of date; nor another, because it is so new, as not yet to appear, whether it is going to be popular. And I hardly know a surer mark of the want of this Christian independence, than great quickness in men to vindicate their freedom from human systems—their independence to think for themselves. Jesus on one occasion spoke to the Jews of their being made free by the truth. They took fire at once at the suggestion, that they were not free, and replied, " We be Abraham's seed, and were never in bondage to any man ; how sayest thou then, Ye shall be made free ? " (John viii. 33.) Indeed, had they forgotten their seventy years' bondage in Babylon ? nay, that they were even then in bondage to the Romans ? Why the very fact, that they were not then politically free, rendered them so sensitive, so quick to vindicate their freedom, that they did not stop to reflect, whether the freedom spoken of by Jesus were not something very different from that, the want of which was so mortifying to their pride. We may still see cases very similar. If men are very quick to vindicate the freedom of their opinions—to assert their independence of thinking as others do, of believing a thing because it has been long or generally believed ; it is a pretty strong indication, that their opinions are not properly their own—that they are slaves to the fear of not being thought liberal-minded.

If a man really feels, that there is none great but God—that it is He who sitteth on the circle of the earth, while the inhabitants thereof are but as grasshoppers—if thus it is his first desire, to believe what He declares, and to do what He commands, esteeming it but a very small matter to be judged of man's judgment, he will be little likely to boast his freedom from being ruled by the opinion of feeble mortals. But, if one has never thrown off the fear of man, so as to resolve in good earnest, that he will think and act, as accountable ultimately to God alone; it is natural, that a secret consciousness of the fear of man, of the slavish dread of being spoken of as illiberal or unfashionable, should render him quick to assert (what he is half conscious may be well disputed) his freedom from being subject to the opinion of others.

This was just the case of the would-be liberals at Corinth. They made great ado about their emancipation from superstition to the freedom of Christianity. The secret was, they were very ambitious of being known as in advance of other Christians. Yet their vaunted independence was but false. It was such a dependence on the popular breath, as led them to make great ado about their attaining to what was indeed but a very small matter; and about which a mind truly liberal and charitable would never have vaunted itself; but rather have said, Have I faith in what I differ from my weaker brethren? I will have it to myself before God. Happy is he, that condemneth not himself in that thing which he alloweth. (Rom. xiv. 22.)

Is there any thing new under the sun? and is not such indeed the temptation common to man? Such thoughts have often occurred to me, from observing, how many, who seem not to be without regard to Christian principle, are always torturing themselves with the inquiry, What will people think or say, if I do so and so? The observation has led me to regard a true Christian independence, as one of the most desirable, and last attained acquisitions. By *Christian independence*, I mean the settled, quiet determination, to have a judgment and conscience of one's own; to adhere thereto strictly, conscious that one's vindication is on high, and never disquieted with the apprehension, what will the world think or say of me?

If such independence were to be found in

proportion as it is professed, we should be an independent people indeed. But alas! where the Spirit of the Lord is, there is liberty, and no where else is perfect freedom found. The very vaunting bespeaks its want. Paul has not rightly declared the temptation spoken of to be common to man, unless it is that which easily besets us. It becomes then each to beware, how easily he may persuade himself, that he is only disregarding needless scruples, and rejecting human authority, when all the while he is soothing his conscience with opiates, and afraid manfully to avow, what he would see to be the truth, if he would but let conscience honestly utter her voice.

Our peculiar political privileges expose us to some peculiar dangers from the common temptation. The freedom, with which every one may form and utter his opinions on all subjects, it must be expected, will often be abused to licentiousness. It will be construed as a freedom to make God's word speak just what the individual pleases, or to reject it altogether, after just what examination he pleases to give it. Many are thrown on the responsibilities of freemen, who really know very little, in what true freedom consists. Such will often be eager to assert their freedom, by hastily denying the plainest declarations of God's word, and what wiser and better men have firmly believed. And while they promise themselves freedom, they are still servants of sin and of a guilty conscience, and slaves to the opinions of men. They are servants of sin. Consciousness of guilt drives them to tax their ingenuity to set aside what God, has plainly declared. And the same tyranny of a guilty conscience hinders them from reposing quietly in their boasted liberty and security. Hence their artifices to conceal their uneasiness. Hence their loud protestations of their ease and confidence for the future; when, if they really felt so, there would be no need of so loudly proclaiming it. Hence, in proportion as a guilty conscience creates a hell within, men are eager to run after every one, who comes to repeat the old story of no hell to be feared hereafter: when, if conscience were really quiet, the stale report would not be thought worth running after.

They who thus understand not, that

He is the freeman, whom the truth makes free,
And all are slaves beside,

are slaves to the opinion of men. Just because

they have not met God on his own terms, settled their account, made their peace with him, and acceded to the terms, on which they are to meet him in judgment; just for this reason, they cannot esteem it a very small matter to be judged of man's judgment: and accordingly their fear of man keeps them back from pursuing seriously the inquiry, how they are to make their calling and election sure, and from seeking truth, wherever it is to be found.

My countrymen, will you thus live, and move, and have your being, in the breath of your fellow creatures of yesterday? Shall the descendants of them, who left their homes to cross an ocean and subdue a wilderness, rather than submit their faith to the established creed—of them, who took up arms at the risk of estate and life, rather than submit to a paltry tax from a foreign power—shall men so descended, so belie their descent, as to suppress or give up their own sober convictions to their equals, who, for aught you know, have never sought the truth with such intensity of desire, as to deserve a moment's regard? Will you not so declare your independence of men, as to consider your salvation of body and soul, as too important a matter to be reached by the fear of their sneers or reproaches ; so that you will quietly refer the vindication of the reasonableness of your conduct to the last tribunal, like one determined to stand or fall to his own master ? This must be your course, if you would stand in that judgment at the last. Nay this must be your course, if you would enjoy here the consciousness, that your peace is not at the mercy of every changing breath.

Modern liberalism (I speak not of the intents of individuals) seems to me to be founded in the desire to repel the charge, that " the carnal mind is enmity against God "—" deceitful above all things, and desperately wicked," and charge back upon God the blame of human guilt and human sufferings. To this end men say and unsay; torture scripture and common sense, resolve abounding wickedness into the peculiar impositions of priestcraft—into the blasting influence of false religion—into the unavoidable imperfection of human nature, which cannot fail of the kind allowance of our heavenly Father ; which is just a softer way of saying, God will acknowledge himself to have so constituted us, that we inevitably commit a quantum of sin, for which he cannot exact a strict account, without forfeiting his character as a kind father—that so far he must acknowledge sin to be no sin, or that its blame rests upon himself.

Thus too God has a controversy with men, as to the many contradictory interpretations and perversions of his word. He insists, that the fault is not in himself; that he has revealed his will plainly, so that the way-faring man, though inexpert, need not err in the way—written so conspicuously, that he may run who reads; that his testimony is sure, making wise the simple; that what is hidden from the wise and prudent, is revealed unto babes in simplicity of desire to learn; that if any man will do his will, he shall know of the doctrine; but if men mistake it, it is because, though the light shines upon the darkness, the darkness admits it not, but men choose darkness rather than light, because their deeds are evil.

But we find men everywhere flatly contradicting all this, and throwing back upon God, the blame, which he charges upon them. They charge him with having written his word so obscurely, that the honest inquirer has no security against the grossest error in interpreting it. Such is the foundation of the papal pretence of the necessity of an infallible interpreter, and the surrender of private judgment. And such precisely is the foundation of modern liberalism; as if God, in professing to give us a clear revelation, had proposed a riddle so obscure, that we must not consider a perverse interpretation of it as an indication of a corrupt heart. I cannot purchase the credit of liberality at the cost of admitting in effect such a charge against my Maker, which he so fully repels. Indeed, tried by pure reason, it seems to me the most unreasonable of pretensions.

But when men reason thus in regard to the soul's concerns, it is natural that they should follow the same analogy in regard to the body; that they should resolve the contraction of the average period of human life to less than one half of three score years and ten, and the frightful aggravation of disease, into the unavoidable frailty of our bodily structure, and the necessary difficulty of arriving at truth as to the prevention and treatment of disease; rather than admit, that God has made very plain and simple the means of fulfilling the number of our days—too plain and simple for corrupt human pride, which would live on the blind veneration of an ignorant and debased multitude. So consistent is our present physical degradation, and the prevalence of unsound minds from unsound bodies, and the

senseless medical superstition which binds so
fast most minds among us, with that liberality
which would relieve man of his consciousness of
guilt, and pretend to consult his true dignity by
repelling God's charge of "deceitful above all
things and desperately wicked," and defying his
curse pronounced against him that trusteth in
man. Awful is the curse we have incurred, by
endeavoring to make out, that it applies only to
man perverted by false religion, or by some
other circumstances betrayed into guilt not common to man.

I do not wonder, that the world is so slow to
admit the conclusions I am urging, while I see
everywhere such a desperate effort to evade the
fundamental principle. This principle is the
indispensable foundation of true charity; not
modern charity, but that which Paul preached
and exemplified. He has sufficiently explained
why, little as he found of satisfaction in the
world, and much as he encountered of groveling
selfishness and ungrateful opposition from those
whose best welfare he was fervently seeking, he
always looked upon the wickedness of men with
" a countenance more in sorrow than in anger."
The world was crucified unto him, and he unto
the world, not by the disappointment of his early

calculations on human virtue and worldly happiness, but by the cross of Christ. (Gal. vi. 14.) He judged, that, if one died for all, then were all dead; and that he died, that they who live, should henceforth live, not unto themselves, but unto him that died for them and rose again. (2 Cor. v. 14, 15.) These passages make the whole matter plain. The mode of man's redemption had taught him to expect to find men everywhere dead in trespasses and sins, at enmity with God, and opposed to the most benevolent efforts for their own welfare. He had found himself to be no exception to the general rule: but though he seemed once to have some real acquiescence in God's character and law, yet when the perfection of that character and law were revealed clearly to his conscience, he found his mistake—that he had been unconscious of enmity against God, only because God had been so wrongly apprehended; that he had always harbored latent propensities to all manner of concupiscence, waiting only a clear view of the purity of God's law, to rouse themselves into action: when this discovery was made, the latent sin revived in its full power—rose up in positive enmity against God, as an active controling reality. (Rom. vii. 8, 9. viii. 7.) Thus was laid the foundation of Paul's charity and forbearance towards the faults of others. The mode of man's redemption, and his acquaintance with his own heart, had taught him to expect to find men everywhere and in all circumstances acting just as he found them : therefore he was not disappointed, nor his temper soured and himself rendered misanthropic.

We see accordingly, that if men take a different view of human nature, when their attention becomes riveted upon one form of wickedness, or when their party spirit is raised against it, they are much more merciless in their denunciations than the Christian, who enters thoroughly into Paul's views. And many who admit into their creed, expressed however strongly in general terms, the confession, that universally the heart of man is deceitful above all things and desperately wicked, still reluct obstinately against fully admitting the same as a sober reality. Thus the denunciations against the unparalleled wickedness of slave-holding, or any other form of depravity, are founded in a deep-rooted determination to get rid of admitting, that we must soberly calculate on finding unrenewed men in all circumstances at enmity with God, and of course at enmity with the best welfare of his creation.

In the fashionable habit too, of courting the praise of liberality, by speaking soft words of popery, I see much to account, why the community is so disposed to go on in the admission of papistical principles in regard to the body.

As a remedy for existing evils, next to that greatest and best of remedies, which the gospel brings to every heart which heartily receives it, I repeat, that "we must abolish all monopolies and mysteries, make the interest and duty of all classes coincide, and have people pay for knowledge rather than be taxed for ignorance." I do not say, into precisely what form these principles should be carried out. One, as that to which we must ultimately arrive, suggests itself to me, that the whole community be divided into associations, each about the size of a common parish, to employ and compensate its physician, with a fixed salary, to lecture on the means of preserving health, and administer to all its sickness: and its lawyer likewise, to attend on the same terms to all the business within his department. It is not extravagant to say, that in such a state of things, sickness would soon be diminished to one twentieth its present amount, human life prolonged again to the average duration of three score years and ten, and nineteen twentieths of the now litigated cases settled in a private way.

But if this condition cannot be brought about at once, there are steps, which we can take towards it. We need not by our votes give the legal profession so large a representation in our legislative assemblies, so beyond its relative importance in the community. We may for the most part keep out of courts of justice, and leave the dependents thereof alone to their honorable business. Public sentiment may exact, that the lawyer's fees shall not depend on the length to which he can protract a case—that the fee shall be settled by agreement with his client beforehand, to depend on success, if the client so exacts. In medicine, if we cannot at once establish the habit of paying for health, and not for sickness, we can demand the immediate repeal of all laws* recognizing a monopoly and exclusive privileges : or we can practically nullify such laws, by showing, that we will not submit to our legislators, what medicine we will take, or what class of physicians employ, more

* This whole volume, (except the Appeal to the legal profession,) was written before the extra-session of the legislature of Massachusetts, in 1835. A few sentences are less fully applicable, than they have been here, and are still in many of the States.

than we will submit to them, what creed we shall believe, or what church attend ; that we mean to have every practitioner estimated, as he can satisfy people of his success in curing, without the slightest regard, whether he is dignified M. D. or not. All the arguments for such laws, are so exactly parallel to what have been used in almost every country for an established church, and for legislation against heresy and schism, and so fully refuted here, that to indicate the comparison is a sufficient refutation.*

I am earnest on this point, because, next to the blessing of that liberty found only where the Spirit of the Lord is, I thank God most heartily for my emancipation from medical superstition ; that I dare use my own eyes to mark the effects

---

* " The condition of a minister is not such as is stated to exist in America, where, as we are assured by a well known and credible minister of that country, ' no minister of any Protestant denomination, to my knowledge, has ever received a sufficient living two years in succession.' "—*Dr. Dealtry's charge, quoted Christian Observer, May,* 1835.

The American minister referred to, is doubtless Mr. Flint, who asserts thus much in regard to the western States. The extension of his remark to the whole country, was but a moderate stretching for a church-and-state advocate.

of medical practice ; and despise the cry *quack-ery* or *empiricism*, when used to frighten people into obedience, and to sustain the credit of the old monopoly, as heartily as I do the cry *heresy* or *illiberality*, when used to deter from free inquiry, or a free expression of opinion in religion.

There is very manifest a restlessness in the community at present ; a deep conviction, that the social system is far behind its perfection ; a disposition to distrust every thing old, and to try every thing new, a groaning and travailing in pain together, as if people were half conscious of a glorious liberty of the children of God, to which they may fairly aspire, and fully conscious of their immense distance from yet reaching it. In such circumstances, I see immense danger of a general rising to sweep away everything old and venerated indiscriminately. To prevent such a catastrophe precisely, I have ventured to give these my thoughts to the public, in which I have attempted to point out, to the best of my ability, where the great evil lies, and to invite all to a cordial co-operation for its correction. I believe there is good sense and generosity enough in the people, to give each profession a fair opportunity yet to correct its own evils ; but if this opportunity is not soon and heartily embraced, I expect to see the people arise in their strength, to take the correction into their own hands. I write, not to urge them to this. That were unnecessary, for the event is inevitable according to the present course of things. But I write, to urge upon those most interested, to avert the danger by removing the just causes of complaint: or, if they will not take warning, that the people may be better instructed, where precisely lies the cause of their grievances, and the impediments to the progress of social improvement, that they may not assail rooted habits and old institutions indiscriminately.

I am sensible that there is a melancholy aspect to the considerations I have presented. Melancholy indeed it is, to see men everywhere leagued together to counteract the benevolent designs of their Creator towards themselves. But the view I have taken seems to me the most cheering and animating which can be taken in the face of obvious facts. If it sets man very low, it vindicates the conduct and word of God. It shows, that our errors and sufferings are not because He made our best welfare either for this life or the life to come, so difficult to be found; but that men have obstinately and inexcusably set themselves against the rules of living prescribed in his word, and against the warnings not to trust our interests to human disinterestedness, perpetually there inculcated, and in his providence also. It shows too that we may anticipate speedily a vast improvement of the social system, without trusting to human virtue to bring it about; that the simple spirit of republicanism, modified only by that degree of disinterested Christian benevolence which may be fairly calculated on, will inevitably bring about the glorious result, and evince, in a stronger sense than has generally been apprehended, that *vox populi* is indeed *vox Dei.* May we then repeat the maxim, not as hitherto too generally, to magnify our own achievements, but to ascribe the kingdom, the power, and the glory, where they are most justly due ; and to ask, with more wondering admiration, What have we that we have not received ? and, Who hath made us to differ ?

I know, that very different anticipations as to the ultimate issue of things are entertained by many, in view of some obvious tendencies to disorganization, to abusing liberty to licentiousness. I cannot but consider these things as incident to our present transition state from an imperfect to a perfect degree of liberty, rather than as evils to be perfected, when republican

principles shall have become fully recognized.
As Paul declares, that "where the Spirit of the
Lord is, there is liberty;" (2 Cor. iii. 17.) so I
believe, that where liberty is—where the shackels
of aristocratic habits and superstition are completely thrown off—there will be the Spirit of the
Lord; there Christianity in its simplicity will
be most cordially received; there men will divest
themselves of false delicacy in regard to religion,
which, like false delicacy in other things, is
most powerful in a transition state; there people
will dare really to think for themselves on religion, instead of being beguiled by the name of so
doing. Where they do so, as conscious of being
left to stand or fall to their own Master, they are
in the readiest way to find that the service of
God is perfect freedom; the uncaviling reception
of his declarations, the best cultivation of the
intellect; and the casting of their crowns at his
feet, their highest exaltation.

I believe we have reached the lowest point of
physical degradation; that the present general
move among people, to inquire how health is to
be preserved and life prolonged, will speedily
issue in results parallel to the strengthened and
cultivated intellects everywhere raised up, when
after the stupor of ages, people resolved to in-

quire for themselves into the means of their spiritual health.

We must indeed calculate on not finding the frailty of man and the shortness and uncertainty of life, so fertile a topic of exhortation, as has hitherto been. But already, how has it ceased to move! How generally has it been confessed, that in the prevalence of the cholera, or other epidemic, instead of learning wisdom from judgments abroad in the earth, men have rather said practically, Let us eat and drink, for to-morrow we die! Now my philosophy of Body and Soul leads me to attribute this insensibility to the language of Providence and to the declarations of revelation, these intellects debased to sense and dead to things unseen, very much to physical causes—to the abominations, with which human stomachs are treated under the names of food and medicine. I anticipate indeed a prolongation of human life to the patriarchal, if not to the antediluvian age : but not a return of antediluvian wickedness; because the means, by which life is to be prolonged, coincide with the self-denying spirit of Christianity. They who expect the result simply from a reform in medicine, or that medical skill at its best estate is to do much towards lengthening life, will inevitably find themselves mistaken. Yet this is evidently the expectation of the reckless portion of the community—the partizans of infidelity and sensuality. Very different were the rules of living, upon the observance of which God promised to the ancient Israelites, " He shall bless thy bread, and thy water; and I will take away sickness from the midst of thee. There shall nothing cast their young, or be barren, in thy land ; the number of thy days (70 years) I will fulfil." (Ex. xxiii. 25, 26.) Indeed I need not the authority of revelation to satisfy me, that such a mode of living, as Moses prescribed, is the only sure means of securing such results.

As the line between them who mean to serve the Lord in body, soul and spirit, and them who mean to live to themselves, is becoming more and more distinct, I am not sure that the final extirpation of wickedness from the earth will not be brought about by a still increasing devotion to appetite, with a corresponding dependence on the stimulating process of repairing for a time the constitution, till the race of the wicked become extinct through want of physical ability for its own continuance. We are not like the antediluvians, with the power of abusing constitutions fitted to run a thousand years.

Hard and self-denying is the process of getting back to any thing nigh where we were. The wisdom learned by this process will be a strong guarantee against a return to the sins, which have brought us where we are.

Thus we might reason, independent of God's express promise, that the time, when in consequence of ceasing to eat swine's flesh, and to practise kindred abominations, (Isa. lxv. 4.) the days of his people shall be prolonged to the age of a tree, (v. 22.) shall be a time of corresponding spiritual prosperity. " And it shall come to pass, that before they call I will answer ; and while they are yet speaking, I will hear. The wolf and the lamb shall feed together, and the lion shall eat straw like the bullock : and dust shall be the serpent's meat. They shall not hurt nor destroy in all my holy mountain, saith the Lord." (vs. 24, 25.)

In the increasing sense of our shameful physical degradation, and the spreading resolution to know and remove the cause, I see one of the surest indications, that "the night is far spent," and "the day is at hand." (Rom. xiii. 12.) I see such an indication in the present groaning and travailing in pain together, as under a bondage to be borne no longer. The increasing light of that day must shame men out of the artifices, at present so often employed, to conceal their life-long bondage through fear of death. It will not require the full blaze of day, to make it very clear, that many betray their subjection to such bondage, by the levity, or by the assurance, with which they assert their freedom from it.

Reader, are you one of those, who profess to have ascertained, that the world of wo is only a bugbear fit to frighten children, and for doting insanity to rave about? Are the fears of a coming judgment the frequent subject of your jest over your cups, or in the merry circle? Now have a care, lest as the intellects of men clear from the clouds arising from abused stomachs, you betray to them more than you would willingly confess: lest it appear too plainly, that you are jesting away your fears.

Suppose you were about sending a boy by night on an errand through some lonely path, that led by a building which popular superstition regarded as a haunted house. You lecture him on the folly of such notions, and exhort him to fear nothing. He promises fairly, and sets out. Now, as he draws near the fearful place, he begins to whistle; and, as he draws nearer still, to jest about goblins and ghosts. Well you see through all this.   He is resolved to have enough of the man not to run like a coward; but yet cannot summon fortitude enough to pass on in quiet dignity.   He must use some artifice to keep up his courage.   He is whistling away his fears.

I have seen very similar conduct in persons of a larger growth, who were children in religious knowledge.   I have witnessed a sporting with the fear of death and the judgment to follow, very inconsistent for men, who had dispassionately and deliberately found that fear to be groundless, but which bore a very strong resemblance to the conduct of the boy jesting away his fears.   Have a care, I repeat, lest, while you laugh at the fears entertained by others of the punishments of a life to come, you do not let out the secret, that you are laughing up your own courage—that you are laughing away your own fears.

If a portion of your neighbors should be seized with such an insanity, as to be continually disquieted by spectres floating before their eyes, the creation of their own imagination, in consequence of which they were never secure to follow their business quietly, or to taste undisturbed any of the enjoyments of life; would it be

characteristic of the sound mind to make a jest
of the imaginary miseries, that others were suffering? Would you not rather suspect, that he
who could thus sport with the pitiable delusion
of his fellows, was either sadly wanting in humanity, or that his own mind began to be in-
fected with the common delusion, and that he
was making his utmost effort to laugh himself
out of it?

Let me then assure you, who affect to laugh
at the fear of a coming judgment, that, however
unseemly the subject be for mirth, while you
profess to regard such fear as groundless, I feel
a sort of satisfaction in seeing you make it a
subject of derision. I take it as an indication,
that you are not sincere—that your conscience
is not so seared, as you would have it believed—
that you cannot set the justice of God at defiance so quietly, as you profess—that your fears
will come in spite of you—and that you would
not be so inhuman, as to deride or reproach
others for tormenting themselves with the fear
of what may follow after death, if you did not
find it necessary to adopt this poor artifice, to
conceal your fears from yourself, and from others
too; like the boy, who jests about goblins in the
dark, to keep up his courage—to jest away his
fears.

One thing is yet wanting to render the suppo-
sitiou I have made parallel with your case.
None less resemble the men tormented with imaginary spectres, none look forward with less
trembling apprehensions, than the Christians,
whom you imagine so bound and tormented by
the fear of hell. If they are deluded, it is a delusion of bright images—a halo around the narrow house, so that no longer to their apprehension do

> Darkness, death, and long despair,
> Reign in eternal silence there.

Your mode of reasoning is such, as seems to
me, no intellect could admit, but from sympathy
with a sadly maltreated stomach. I therefore
look to physical improvement as the great and
effectual means of exposing its inconclusiveness.

The indications, that the long night of superstition and ignorance, of mental, moral, and
physical degradation is far spent, and that day
in its best sense is at hand, should serve to all
as a powerful incitement, to cast away the works
of darkness, and to put on the armor of light.
The day promised is such as shall try men's
souls—try them beyond the trial, to which they
have been put by the former great developments

of republican principles. In the very want of faith, now prevalent, to apprehend the promises of the final reign of truth and righteousness on the earth, I seem to see a sign of the Son of man's speedy coming. (Luke xviii. 8.) If they who are essentially prepared for his coming, need to be aroused from their sleep, to prepare to welcome him, how shall fare the remaining multitude yet dead in trespasses and sins? And what voice shall effectually warn them to meet him, who is like a refiner's fire, and like fuller's soap? If the amount of temptation common to man has hitherto proved sufficient to entice the many into the broad way that leadeth to destruction, and to leave to the few the narrow way that leadeth unto life; how shall it be in the last great trial preparatory to the final establishment of the Son of God in his kingdom upon earth?

Reader, I would fain add a word to beat you off from the old cavil, that your heavenly Father will surely provide, that so many of his creatures shall not be lost by trials, which himself had ordained with full fore-knowledge of the result. I would fain show you, that this plea not only contradicts his express word, but really charges the guilt of your sins upon him. I have endeavored to convict you of carrying on a controversy with your Maker in regard to the life that now is, of being deluded by fashion into using the engines of death as the means of life—all in defiance of the plain word of God, and the evidence of your own eyes. The conviction I should little value, unless it lead you to inquire, whether it be not even so for the life that is to come.

Do not inquire why God does not force the soul's salvation upon you, any more than the health of the body, in despite of your negligence, or your efforts to destroy both. You may see the reason fully, if landed at last on the Rock of ages, you look back on these temptations and dangers, and around on the ruins of a world, w .h feelings akin to those, with which the mariner, hardly escaped from shipwreck, climbs the ocean's bank, and turning sees his fellows still laboring hopelessly beneath the tempest. And the painful spectacle is not without its pleasure: not that he delights in the calamity of others; but because the sight gives him a keener apprehension of his own security. That similar may be the feelings, with which every reader shall survey the last great wreck, is the fervent prayer of the writer.

CPSIA information can be obtained
at www.ICGtesting.com
Printed in the USA
BVHW03s1738020518
515046BV00016B/214/P